D0288024

Training Young Horses

A PONY CLUB PUBLICATION

Training
Young Horses

THE BRITISH HORSE SOCIETY
and THE PONY CLUB

© The British Horse Society 1989

Compiled by the Pony Club Training
Committee to replace *Training the Young
Horse and Pony,* which was first published
by the British Horse Society in 1961.

Designed by Alan Hamp

Illustrations by Fiona Silver
Photographs by Elizabeth Furth
  and Kit Houghton

Published by The Pony Club

Designed and produced by
Threshold Books,
The Kenilworth Press Limited,
661 Fulham Road, London SW6 5PZ

Typeset by Computerised Typesetting
Services Ltd, Redhill, Surrey
Printed in Great Britain by Westway Offset,
Wembley

**British Library Cataloguing in
Publication Data**
Training Young Horses
  1. Livestock: Horses. Training
  I. Pony Club, Training Committee
  036.1'083
  ISBN 0 900226 37 4

Contents

List of illustrations   6

1 Introduction   7

2 Breeding   13

3 Feeding the In-foal Mare and Youngstock   25

4 Foals   32

5 Yearlings, Two- and Three-Year-Olds   43

6 Lungeing   55

7 Backing   72

8 Riding Away   81

9 Teaching the Horse to Jump   88

10 Widening the Horse's Experience   101

Index   109

List of Illustrations

Frontispiece   6
Bucking for his life   9
Mares and foals   13
Figs.1a-f Stages of foaling   19-21
Growth from foetus to foal   25
The foal   32
Fig.2 Catching the foal   34
Fig.3 The Dutch foal slip   36
Fig.4 Leading the foal   36
Fig.5 Returning to the stable   38
The yearling   43
The two-year-old   46
Fig.6 The roller   48
Fig.7 Introducing the blanket   49
The three-year-old   51
Fig.8 Gently opening his
    mouth   54
On the lunge   55
Figs.9a-c The lungeing
    cavesson   56
Fig.10 Stirrups fastened up   58
Fig.11 Side reins to girth
    straps   58
Fig.12 The correct bend   60
Figs.13a-b The horse's
    outline   61
Figs.14a-d Position of the
    lunger   62

Fig.15 Holding the lunge line   63
Fig.16 Leading, ready to
    lunge   65
Fig.17 Teaching the horse to
    lunge   69
Backing   72
Fig.18 Lungeing before
    backing   73
Figs.19a-c Stages of
    backing   76-7
Fig.20 Accepting the rider   79
Riding away   81
Fig.21 The 'open rein'   82
Fig.22 Over a ground pole   86
Jumping   88
Figs.23a-c Schooling fences   90
Fig.24 Building a 'runner'   91
Fig.25 Tracks when lungeing   91
Fig.26 Jumping on the lunge   92
Fig.27 Trotting over poles   94
Figs.28a-e The phases of
    the jump   95-6
Fig.29 His first jump   98
Fig.30 Becoming more
    competent   99
Out and about   101
Figs.31-3 The joy of riding
    him   106

1

Introduction

Training the Young Horse and Pony was first published in
1961. It was a textbook designed to help members of the Pony
Club to train or to improve their ponies. It is now replaced by
this book, *Training Young Horses*, which has been expanded
to cover the choice of mare and stallion, and the care of the
in-foal mare, the mare and foal, and youngstock.

The training programme described begins with the handling of the newly born foal and follows through to the schooling of the young horse.

For the sake of clarity, subjects such as lungeing and
jumping are dealt with in separate chapters. These should be
used at all the appropriate stages of training, so that they
become integral parts of the horse's general education.

The classical ideas used in Pony Club teaching have been
retained, but the book gives a more comprehensive guide at
each stage of training, and explains the use of contemporary
facilities and equipment.

*Reading a book can never be a substitute for experience.
Members will need expert help to handle, back and train
young horses, and with the care of mares and foals.* In time
and with considerable experience, some members will
become expert and, as Instructors, will be able to show these
skills to the younger generation.

The trainer
Breeding a foal or acquiring a very young animal, guiding his
progress, and watching him grow into a mature, well-
schooled horse, can be a most rewarding experience. The

7

subject is trained from his raw state and the responsibility for the outcome lies with the the trainer – you!

To be a good trainer you must have knowledge, skill, patience, sympathy and nerve. You must be quiet, determined, good-tempered, tactful and self-disciplined.

You must be an experienced rider, with the knowledge to guide and teach the horse through each stage of his development.

You should understand enough of how a horse's mind and body work to recognise when he is mentally and physically capable, and has the necessary condition and muscular fitness to do what is asked of him.

Be prepared to adapt your plans for the individual animal. The suggested programme should be used as a guide, bearing in mind that every horse is different and cannot be expected to respond or make progress in the same way. Differences in conformation and condition alone will mean that lessons which are easy for some may be difficult, tiring, or even painful, for others.

Teach only one new lesson at a time. Reaffirm previous lessons then 'make haste slowly'.

If things go wrong blame yourself, not the horse: 'There are no bad horses, only bad horsemen'!

Psychology – the mind of the horse

Before attempting to train a horse, it is important to know something of how his mind works.

Originally, horses and ponies survived in their wild state because they could escape quickly from their enemies. Unlike other animals which when attacked go to ground, run up a tree, or turn and fight, horses found safety in fleeing from their enemies. To warn them of danger, they developed acute senses and very quick reactions. When unsure and worried they needed to be especially sensitive. In the past, the water-hole was a dangerous place for wild horses because predators could strike while concentration was lost as the horses were drinking. A moment's hesitation or separation from the herd might have left the horse kicking his way to freedom from an attack by wolves, or bucking for his life to dislodge the claws of a puma who had sprung on to his back.

We are therefore dealing with an extremely nervous animal who has a strong herding instinct, whose chance of survival originally lay in effective bucking, kicking and ability to move off at speed. Even now, these are the three instinctive reactions of a frightened or excited horse.

Bucking for his life.

As well as being used for eating, a horse's mouth, sometimes in conjunction with his lips and muzzle, serves as his 'hands'. He uses it to hold and move things, to scratch, and to communicate. If he is angry, irritated or spoiled, he can be vicious with it. Though he must learn that biting is bad manners, we must realise why he is biting and be firm but

9

fair. For example, thin-skinned or sensitive horses will habit-
ually bite during grooming and when being girthed up. They
must not be allowed to bite you, but you should use a softer
brush when grooming, and you must be extremely careful
never to pinch their skin when girthing up.

Horses have very limited reasoning power but excellent
memories. They frequently remember places, roads and
other horses. Young native ponies who have suffered during
round-ups – particularly from rough handling by men – may
be perfectly normal in their attitudes towards women and
children, but will be mistrustful of men for the rest of their
lives.

A horse is taught by associating certain facts in his mind,
in a simple, clear way. Good behaviour becomes associated
with comfort and reward. Devious behaviour is associated
with instant correction. In this way, good behaviour becomes
a habit. Fortunately the horse is a creature of habit and, once
they are established, habits such as coming to call and standing still while the rider mounts, become almost instinctive.
For this reason, bad habits such as barging into the trainer
when he opens the stable door, must be stopped immediately.
The horse must be taught respect for the human and must
learn to move back from the door when anyone enters the
stable. Unless the correction is made firmly and quickly, this
type of bad habit will become established, and will be
extremely difficult to break.

Horses are gregarious by nature, and they like to imitate
each other. Use can be made of this by, for example, introducing the young horse to traffic and to going out hunting in the
company of an experienced, well-behaved companion. In
calmer circumstances he must learn to work without the
comfort of his friends.

The horse enjoys eating, resting and running free. It is not
natural for him to be confined within four close walls. He may
become bored or nervous and may develop stable vices, such
as weaving, unless he can see what is happening outside, or

has something else to interest him during his unoccupied time.

The young horse will learn to enjoy the security of consistent, regular and sympathetic handling. Pain and confusion make him nervous and his instinct then is to buck, kick and run away. He has little hope of understanding us unless we understand him. His feelings and emotions must be recognised so that his actions can be anticipated. You must communicate clearly what you would like him to do. If he does not obey, you must be aware of the reason, recognising the difference between nervousness and misunderstanding or naughtiness. You must act accordingly. When the horse obeys, you must reward him immediately. In this way he will soon learn to enjoy pleasing his trainer, and the beginning of a lasting rapport and trust will have been established.

Training

In training we make use of the horse's faculties to smell, see, hear and feel. We develop his confidence by moving placidly, speaking soothingly and stroking him quietly but firmly. At the same time, he must from the beginning learn to respect and to become obedient to his trainer. For example, you must not allow him to trample over you or pester you too much with his muzzle. A firm 'No' and a light slap will be easily understood. You should then reward him with a pat or a kind word for stopping his bad habit; and then change the subject. Reward and correction must be instantaneous, so that they are associated clearly with the horse's preceding move. Never punish a horse in temper or out of spite.

Tact, common-sense and timing are also important. For example, before teaching him to stand still, wait for a calm day when he is well worked, and quiet. Do not try to teach him to stand while a noisy wind blows leaves around his feet. New lessons should be taught at the 'right' moment, which is usually when the horse is working in a quiet, obedient way, but is not tired.

If lessons are made too difficult, a young horse may become

devious, and quick to use his superior strength to evade the wishes of his trainer. If the work is too repetitive he may become bored and lose interest. The trainer must know by the horse's expression and from the way he is working how he is feeling; whether he is relaxed, tense, finding the work hard or easy; trying hard or starting to be obstinate. The trainer must see what is happening, know what to do about it and communicate clearly with the horse. For example, you must praise the horse while good work is being performed, ask for more effort at a sensible moment, and be able to divert his attention to avoid or correct a disobedience before it is fully developed.

If things go wrong, be patient. Keep calm and always be prepared to go back and reaffirm the previous lesson.

By consistency in communication the horse learns to understand what he is required to do, and that obedience will result in comfort and security. He develops good manners at all times; at first in the stable and while outside 'in hand' and on the lunge. Later he is 'backed' and learns to carry his rider in an easy, balanced and sure-footed way. With correct guidance, he becomes a pleasure to ride.

As he matures, his work is planned to develop his mental and physical powers. He must understand your wishes and obey them to the best of his ability. In return, you must accept his limitations, help him through his difficulties and allow him to share your pleasure when he has performed well.

2

Breeding

Breeding a foal for yourself to ride can be an interesting experience, covering a wide area of fresh subject matter.

The responsibility of choosing a stallion for your mare, and of managing her and then her offspring throughout his formative years, will all broaden your knowledge and experience.

Facilities required

Broodmares and growing youngstock require safe pastures with some shelter. They all need sufficient quality grazing with a variety of herbage, but the requirements of the Thoroughbred and TB crosses are greater than those of the hardier mountain and moorland ponies.

Broodmares should not run out with geldings; they will be happier in the company of other mares.

It is natural for a mare to have her foal in privacy. She will try to find a quiet place for herself, and will probably foal in the early hours of the morning. Therefore, shortly before the foaling date it will be safer to put her in a field on her own so that if she should drop her foal while out in the field, she will not be disturbed and the foal will come to no harm. The field should be fresh and clean, with safe and obvious fencing. Wire is especially hazardous.

The field should not contain ponds, streams, ditches or hollows into which the foal could fall. A safe trough of fresh water must be available.

In the early days after birth the mare and foal need time to adjust to each other in peace and quiet. Once their rapport is established, the ideal situation would be to introduce another mare and foal, so that the mares are left in peace and quiet whilst their foals play together.

A large loosebox, depending on the size of the mare, will be required. 12 ft × 14 ft (3.6 m × 4.2 m) are the minimum dimensions required for a mare up to 15.2 hh. At some time or another, a situation may occur when it will be necessary for them both to come in, even if you choose to let the mare foal outside. The box should have a well-drained, flat floor and should be deeply bedded with no buckets or projections which may hinder or harm the foal.

The mare

Before the breeding from your mare, consider the following:

☐ *Soundness.* She should be free from hereditary defects. Your veterinary surgeon should check her for soundness and suitability.

☐ *Ability.* She should have proved herself a good sensible ride and useful in some way.

☐ *Conformation.* Her general make and shape should be satisfactory for the planned purpose.

☐ *Size.* She should be capable of producing the height of animal you require (13.2 hh × 15.2 hh does not automatically produce 14.2 hh).

☐ *Temperament.* A sensible, generous temperament is all-important. The mare will affect the foal by her example and by heredity.

□ *History*. Check that her stud record, if any, her age and her pedigree are satisfactory.

Having considered the important part that your mare will play, and having formed a very clear picture of the end product you would like, choose a suitable stallion.

The stallion

The choice is wide and the result will be permanent. Take time and trouble to choose the right stallion. If a pure-bred, make sure he is a good example of that particular breed. He should, as described above for the mare, be sound, have ability and the conformation, size and temperament required. Look also for the special qualities which should add to those of your particular mare. The best indication of a stallion's worth are his progeny.

Finally, remember that your foal will be worth more if he is eligible for registration either as a pure-bred or even part-bred in a recognised society.

While you are looking at the stallion, take the opportunity of inspecting the stud to check the conditions in which the mare will be kept when she visits the stallion.

Sending the mare to stud

The best time for your foal to be born is in early summer, so the mare should go to stud in late spring.

Arrangements should be made as early as possible with the stud of your choice, who will advise you regarding their swabbing requirements. Two separate swab tests are normally requested:

(1) A clitoral swab, for contagious equine metritis. This must be carried out by a veterinary surgeon through a Ministry-approved laboratory. A certified result generally takes a week. The mare need not be in season when this swab is taken. The certificate will be required before the mare is accepted at stud.

(2) A cervical swab, taken from the mare when she is in season, to test against venereal diseases. This test can be completed by your own veterinary surgeon in 48 hours. Many studs insist on carrying out this test themselves before the mare is served. If you do not know when she is in season, make arrangements for her to go to stud at least three weeks before your would like her covered. Alternatively, she should be swabbed at home and sent to stud a week before she is due in season. Your mare will benefit from a week at stud before coming into season, during which time she will acclimatise and settle down.

The gestation period is 11 months. To calculate the best time to send your mare to the stallion, work backwards from when you would prefer the foal to be born. The mare will come into season (cycle) every 21 days. The season lasts approximately 5 days, during which time she should ovulate and be receptive to the stallion. If she conceives, she will not come into season 21 days later and will reject the stallion at that time. If she 'turns' she will not have 'held' to the stallion and must be covered again. It is therefore preferable to leave her at the stud until after her next 'season' is due.

You will be expected to present the mare at stud in a healthy condition, with tetanus and equine influenza cover. Her hind shoes should be removed. So that she can be identified, she should have a clearly marked, well-fitting, headcollar. Most studs give an anti-worm preparation to every mare on arrival.

The mare due to foal at stud
If the mare is in foal, and due to foal at the stud, she must arrive there one month before the due date, so that she can acquire the necessary immunities to this strange environment, which will be vital to the well-being of her foal.

The mare due to foal at home
If she has a foal at foot, the mare will come back into season –

16

her foaling heat – approximately one week after foaling. If she is to go to stud with her foal at foot, it is sensible to wait until her next season before putting her to a stallion again. By then the mare will have fully recovered from foaling, and the foal will be stronger, and better able to cope with a different environment and new experiences.

After visiting the stallion
The mare should return home with a certificate giving the date of service and approximate date of foaling. As long as care is taken, and if she does not have a foal at foot, she may return to light work for the next four or five months. She will require no special feeding at this stage. Whether in light work or not she must be kept in healthy condition, but not fat. As the days shorten and the feed value of the grass diminishes, supplementary feeding will become necessary.

The ideal situation for a mare in foal during the winter months is to stable her at night and turn her out in a paddock during the day. Moorland and native ponies will winter out in suitably situated sheltered fields, but must be checked and fed daily.

Signs that the mare is in foal
The first indication that the mare may have 'held' (i.e. is in foal) is if she rejects the stallion when her next 'season' occurs. Further checks may be made as follows:

☐ Ultra-sound scanning can be carried out as early as 21 days. Its advantage is that twins (which are undesirable since they can cause complications) can be detected and aborted in time for the mare to conceive again the same year.
☐ An internal examination by a specialist veterinary surgeon can be made from after about 35 days.
☐ A blood test can be carried out at approximately 60–90 days.
☐ A urine test can be performed at approximately 120 days.

External signs that the mare is in foal will not be seen until after 5½ months, when the foetus is making appreciable growth. From then there may be a gradual change in the shape of the abdomen, but this should not be confused with gross condition. Viewed from behind, the shape of the abdomen may be uneven, showing more one side than the other. Later the belly-line will drop considerably, behind the girth. However, these signs are difficult to detect, and even experts can be misled. A positive sign of a live foal is when it can be seen moving, which will be during the last two months. The movement is apparent low down behind the last rib, just in front of the stifle, and is particularly noticeable immediately after the mare has had a drink.

The tenth month
Within the last month, the mare's belly-line will drop more noticeably and her udder will 'bag up' in preparation for feeding the foal.

Very much nearer her time you may see wax tips, like little clusters of grapes, form on the end of her teats. The muscles on her rump will be come slack, making the backbone prominent and giving the quarters the appearance of being poor.

During the last few weeks, feeds should be reduced in size and it is advisable to give a small bran mash as the last feed at night.

Where to foal
It is acceptable for native ponies to foal out of doors without help, if the weather is fine. The advantages are that the mare will have plenty of space and can have her foal quietly and naturally. Occasionally, especially with larger animals, human assistance can be vital. For this reason it is more practical for larger mares to foal in roomy looseboxes where they can be observed.

Most mares are very secretive, preferring to foal in the early hours, when all is quiet. Their desire for privacy must be respected.

Foaling (Figs. 1a–f)

There are no hard and fast indications as to exactly when the mare is going to foal as all mares are different, but generally the imminent signs are little changes in habits, lengthening of the vulva, increased restlessness, especially disturbed bedding, and finally breaking out in a sweat.

The mare will go to some lengths to foal without help. Supervision should therefore be *very* discreet. Assistance should be on hand at any moment but should not cause the mare any anxiety.

Most mares foal easily, usually lying down, sometimes getting up and down more than once during labour, if things are not quite to their liking. First, the waters break (a gush of fluid), then the mare will rest awhile. Next, the mare will push hard, and first one forefoot and then the second will appear, soon followed by the nose. The head and shoulders will come through with a little more effort, and often the

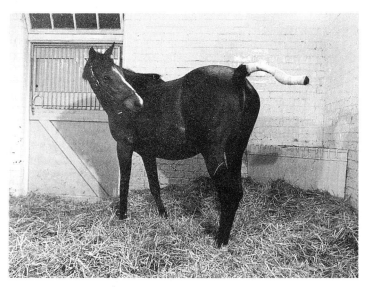

Fig. 1a Becoming restless.

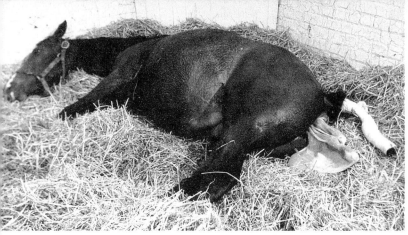

Fig. 1b First one forefoot and then the other will appear.

Fig. 1c The amnion usually breaks naturally, enabling the foal to breathe.

Fig. 1d Born, but still receiving vital blood from his mother.

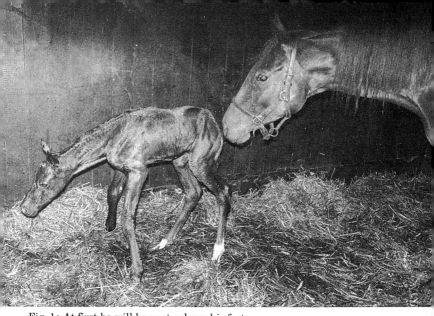

Fig. 1e At first he will be unsteady on his feet.

Fig. 1f One day old.

mare will then take another rest. During this stage, or if no rest is taken and the whole foal comes out, it may be necessary to ensure that the amnion (membrane) covering the the foal's nose has been broken, and the fluid released, so that he can breathe.

The mare should foal no longer than thirty minutes after the waters have broken. If after twenty minutes no progress has been made, *help should be sought.*

After the birth the mare must be left in peace again, so that her activities do not cause the umbilical cord to be broken too soon, because at this stage the foal will be receiving through it a vitally important blood transfusion from his mother.

Left alone, the mare will get to her feet in her own time and the umbilical cord, by then reduced in size, will break naturally. The navel stump should be treated with whatever medication your vet has supplied.

The mare will lick the foal clean and dry, forming a mother-bond with her offspring. This also serves to calm her, encourages her milk to come down, and she is more likely to allow the foal to suckle without being fussy.

Within the next few hours, the placenta (afterbirth) should come away; this is known as 'cleansing'. When it does, it must be checked to see that it is complete, showing two horns of the uterus, both closed at the tips. Place it in a bucket of water so that it may be examined by a vet. If in the meantime the placenta is trailing on the ground behind the mare it should be folded up out of the way and tied with string. Apart from this, do not interfere with it, as it must come away naturally. If the mare has not cleansed within four hours, or if part of the placenta has been retained, it will cause infection in the mare, which is very serious. Therefore the vet must be notified.

During this time, the foal will try to stand up. He will topple over a few times, but will eventually struggle to his feet, find the mare's udder, and begin to suck. Occasionally you may have to steer him in the right direction. He might also need help if the mare is ticklish, and she may have to be held and calmed down with a soothing voice.

The foal *must* receive this early milk, which is called colostrum. It contains all the antibodies which he needs for survival. This is so important that if problems should arise the mare must be milked so that the foal can be bottle-fed.

When the mare and foal are settled and the foal is sucking, remove the sodden straw, and set the bed fair with as little disturbance as possible. Leave the mare with a bran mash and a bucket of water, safely out of reach of the foal. Hay is best fed off the floor. A haynet is dangerous.

If the mare has foaled unobserved, remember to check the afterbirth, treat the foal's navel, and ensure that the foal is sucking, as described above.

Within the first day, the colostrum will help the foal to open his bowels and pass dark, thick, preliminary droppings (meconium). If this does not happen, veterinary help will be needed. Later droppings will change in colour to yellow, which shows that the milk has been digested.

About a week later, when the mare comes back into season, her hormone change may cause the foal to scour. It should not be confused with an infectious scour, which can occur as early as two or three days after birth. In this case the foal will become dehydrated, which is very serious and must be treated promptly by your vet. When any scouring occurs, the foal must be washed clean with a mild soap, rinsing well and ensuring that he is dry. Talcum powder or baby oil should be used to keep the skin from becoming sore.

Check list
☐ The mare must be immunised against tetanus and influenza. Ideally her last booster injection should be given two

months before her foaling date, but in any case it should not be given later than one month before foaling.

☐ Worming advice is best given by your vet, as some wormers are dangerous for in-foal mares, but she should have been wormed regularly and no later than one month before her foaling date.

☐ Some weeks before foaling, her udder should be washed with mild, soapy water and thoroughly dried. Care should be taken to acclimatise her to the feeling of being nudged in this area. With a maiden mare this may take some time.

☐ Contact your vet and advise him that your mare is near her time. Ask for a suitable spray or dressing for the foal's umbilical stump.

☐ Ensure that the box is always spotlessly clean and have a fresh bale of straw or shavings close at hand for a quick change of bedding.

☐ Immediately before foaling it is sensible to bandage up the mare's tail so that it does not get in the way during foaling, or become badly soiled.

☐ Put ready:
Antibiotic spray or dressing for the umbilical stump.
A length of binder twine to tie up the placenta.
Bran for a mash.
A clean bucket (to be filled with warm water) and soap, for washing.

☐ Have available for use in emergencies:
Clean towels to rub the foal dry.
A baby's feeding bottle and teat.
A rug for the mare.
A small woollen blanket for the foal.

If the mare rejects the foal, dies in foaling, or has no milk, the National Foaling Bank will help and advise. If the foal dies, the same organisation may be able to inform you of an orphan foal in need of a foster mother. Your vet will be the best source of help and information.

3

Feeding the In-foal Mare and Youngstock

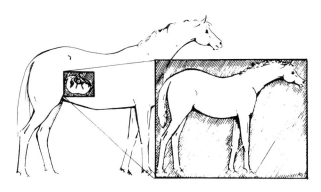

The rapid growth from the five-month foetus to a foal at weaning time.

The subject of feeding, with detailed guides of types and amounts of feeds, is set out in the Pony Club *Manual of Horsemanship*.

The traditional rules of feeding always apply, but additional considerations must be taken into account when feeding in-foal mares, foals and youngstock.

Your aims are for steady growth, with muscles developing on a strong skeletal frame.

The youngster should not be forced into excessively fast development by being over-fed with protein. Neither should he be produced in fat condition, which will put too much strain on immature and fast-growing bones. Fat mares often

25

produce small weak foals, and are certainly difficult to get in foal.

The growth rate of the embryo during the last five months is from something roughly the size of a Jack Russell terrier to a full-term foal. The foal continues this rapid growth from birth to six months old, attaining approximately 50% of the amount he will grow between birth and maturity. This gives an indication of the nutritional quality of the mare's milk. The sheer quantity that she has to produce, which can be 3–4 gallons (13–18 litres) a day, is a considerable drain on her resources. Her well-being is vitally important, so she must be fed appropriately. During the next six months a further 25% of this growth will be achieved, so that at one year old, 75% of the height growth will have taken place. The young horse will not be mature, with his bones fully grown and hardened, until he is at least five years old, more often seven years old.

The best way of feeding is the natural way: grazing on established, quality pasture containing a variety of good grasses and a bottom rich in small herbs. It must be fresh and clean and of adequate acreage. Fresh water and a salt lick will be the only additions to grass needed in the early summer. As this ideal situation may not be readily available – and in any case the value of the grass will decline as the summer progresses – you must understand something of modern feedstuffs and the nutritional value of food so that you can supplement or replace nutriments which are lacking in the grass.

Good-quality hay is the best substitute for grass as the basis of the diet. It provides a large percentage of the roughage required, and may be fed *ad lib* unless the animal is overweight. Proprietary brands of stud cubes and mixes are convenient forms of concentrated feeds. Traditional feeding of oats, barley, bran, chaff, etc, is also recommended, but care must be taken to feed a balanced diet. Good-quality cubes and mixes are produced to contain the necessary feed value and a correct balance of all the vitamins and minerals that the animals will need. The manufacturers recommend how much should be fed, either in a leaflet or printed on the back of the sack.

Different mixes and cubes are available for the various stages of pregnancy, lactation, weaning and for youngstock. It is particularly important to feed the appropriate mix for mares during the last 90 days of pregnancy, during lactation and for foals at weaning time.

The principles
• *Clean fresh water must be available at all times.* The body of the young horse contains 70–80% water; in the adult it is 60%. Horses normally require up to 12 gallons (54 litres) a day, but broodmares and lactating mares will require more. Whilst a horse can lose almost all his body fat and half the body protein without serious ill-effect, a 20% loss of water can be fatal. It is important to check water in field tanks very regularly in summer, to ensure that it is constantly clear and not green with algae. Ice must be broken during frosty weather.
• *Feed little and often.* This rule is essential if the horse is to gain most value from his food. Two factors are all-important:
  1. The stomach of a horse is relatively small, 1¾–3 gallons (8–14 litres) in capacity, depending on the size of the animal. The volume of food eaten will double by the time it reaches the stomach, due to the addition of digestive juices. When it is about two-thirds full, digestion is at its most efficient.
  2. The food passes along the alimentary canal by rhythmical muscular contractions (peristalsis), which require a constant supply of food to be maintained.
• *Feed adequate roughage.* This is the basis of any diet and keeps the alimentary canal active and healthy. It helps the digestive juices act on the concentrates which would otherwise form an indigestible solid mass.

• *Introduce any changes of diet gradually.* For safe and efficient digestion of feeds, any changes should be made gradually. This will allow time for the necessary digestive juices and bacteria to develop.

• *Feed clean and good-quality forage.* This is vitally important at the time rapid growth is taking place. Feeding substandard forage is not only wasteful but can inhibit growth and may cause permanent damage to your mare and foal.

• *Read the labels on proprietary brands of feeds and supplements.* Check the date stamp and follow the directions to avoid feeding an unbalanced diet. Over-supplementation or unbalanced supplementation will result in abnormal growth.

• *Feed according to type, size and physical condition.* Whilst the hardy pony will thrive on a natural diet with little or no supplement, horses and quality animals will require a diet of higher nutritional value.

Use your eye to check the physical condition of your stock. Modify the diet accordingly.

Essential nutrients in the diet
Carbohydrates. These provide the fuel to run the body: the energy for growth and development, body functions, activity and warmth. They are found in cellulose (grass, forage and hay, in which form they make up the larger part of the diet – generally up to 70%), starch (cereals) and sugar (molasses). Feeding hay *ad lib* is a safe way of ensuring that the animal has all the carbohydrates he requires for maintenance, but a mare in foal will need extra in the form of concentrates. Later in pregnancy, concentrates should be gradually increased and roughage decreased.

Proteins. These are for body-building and repair and are found in every living cell in the body. They are present in most foodstuffs, in forage, more so in cereals, and particularly in milk.

Protein requirements differ according to the stage of growth and workload. As a guide, the total protein requirement in the diet to maintain body condition is 8.5%. The requirements of a pregnant broodmare during her last 90 days, when the foetus is growing very quickly, may be double that. The fast-growing foal will require even more, all of which at first is provided in the mare's milk.

Care must be taken not to over-feed ponies, who may be prone to laminitis.

Minerals. These are necessary for all body processes, and are present in varying quantities in good-quality basic feeds. They are considered in two groups, major elements and trace elements:

• Major elements include calcium and phosphorus, which combine with vitamin D and must be correctly balanced to produce good bone development.

Sodium, chlorine and potassium are major elements which are referred to as 'tissue salts' (electrolytes) and are essential for the regulation of body fluids.

Sodium and chlorine combined (sodium chloride) is common salt, most conveniently fed in the form of a mineral lick or rock salt. Potassium is found in the low herbal growth in quality pasture, in tree bark, wood and cider vinegar.

• Trace elements are no less important, but are required in very small amounts. They include iron and copper, essential for healthy blood.

Minerals assimilated by the mare will be passed on to her foal through the milk.

If you are feeding traditional feed (oats, barley, bran, chaff, etc.), a supplement is vital. To be safe, feed a wide-spectrum vitamin/mineral supplement specially manufactured for breeding stock. Check that the calcium, phosphorus and vitamin D are adequate for the stage of pregnancy, lactation or growth. You may need to add extra calcium in the form of limestone flour, depending on the content of your feed and the size of the mare. The calcium and phosphorus requirements of an in-foal mare will, by the end of pregnancy and during lactation, increase to about double that required for normal maintenance.

Vitamins. Growing and breeding horses require vitamins in different quantities from those needed by the adult horse for basic well-being. The appropriate supplement is necessary, care being taken to avoid an imbalance and to follow the

TABLE 1. Fat-soluble vitamins, their uses and sources.

Vitamin	Used for	Found in
A	Vision; growth; reproduction; formation of tissue	Natural herbage and carrots
D (harmful if acquired in excess)	Bone structure	Sunshine, absorbed through the coat; cod liver oil (short shelf-life); unnecessary in summer
E	Quality of muscle structure; fertility	Green forage and hay
K	Blood-clotting	Green forage and hay

TABLE 2. Water-soluble vitamins, their uses and sources.

Vitamin	Used for	Produced by
B group	Utilisation of food and correct functioning of the nervous system	Bacterial action on green food and forage in the gut
C	Correct functioning of the blood and blood vessels throughout the body, interacting with the trace elements iron and copper; defence mechanism	Bacterial action in the gut

instructions given. High-quality pasture and sunshine supply some of them, and the bacterial action in the gut manufactures others. There are two groups of vitamins:

1. Fat-soluble vitamins – namely A, D, E and K, which can be stored in the body fat.
2. Water-soluble vitamins – namely the B group and C, which are required daily.

4

Foals

From the moment that the foal is born, his education has begun and it is your responsibility to produce a confident, level-headed, well-mannered and happy horse.

The foal will quickly learn that he can rely on his mother for comfort and reassurance. He feeds from her and takes pleasure from the feel of her nuzzling him and talking to him. He will follow her with confidence. The mare will discipline the foal, correcting him by laying back her ears, nipping him, or even threatening to kick if he does not behave. Understanding this, you will be able to build up a similar relationship with him. Rubbing his neck and back can be extended gradually to grooming and picking up his feet. Soon you will feed and water him. Your voice can comfort, encourage and reward; it can also reprimand. Remember that reward and correction must be instantaneous, so that they are associated with the appropriate actions.

Psychology
For the first few days of their lives foals are fairly self-confident and curious. As the nervous system develops, and their senses become established, they will be much more sensitive to touch, and shyness will be evident. They are easily frightened, quite unpredictable, quick-thinking and fast to react. They will assimilate commands and generally co-operate – but until their understanding develops you will have to repeat each lesson from the beginning each time that you see them, until it is firmly established. Mentally, they will soon assess you and try to take advantage. They learn bad habits readily. Beware of little actions or tricks which may be amusing at the time, but could be annoying or even dangerous as the foal grows and becomes stronger.

Education
It is essential for you to gain the trust and respect of your foal if you are to have a worthwhile and rewarding partnership in the future. They are all individuals and may need handling in slightly different ways.
• Plan each lesson thoroughly in your mind but be prepared to be flexible to suit the occasion, and the learning rate.
• Handle the youngster firmly and kindly.
• Always move slowly and confidently. Talk soothingly and with warmth, especially to reassure the mare, who may be very foal-proud and protective.
• Whatever happens, keep calm, be consistent, be generous with praise, and never lose your temper.

Throughout the first six months, the dam (his mother) will be your greatest helper. During this time the lessons will be:
☐ To accept handling.
☐ To lead in hand.

Foals

☐ To learn stable manners and handling for grooming, veterinary attention and the farrier.
☐ An introduction to tying up.
☐ To learn about the outside world.
☐ To travel in a horsebox (only if for some good reason this becomes necessary).

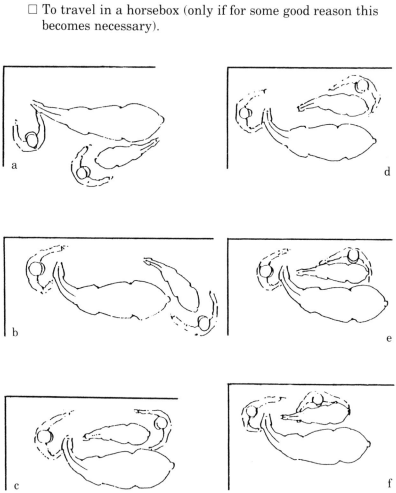

Fig. 2 Catching the foal.

The first day
It is very important to ensure that for the first twenty-four hours the mare and foal are allowed peace and quiet to get to know one another. The mare may be very possessive or anxious, so it is essential for you to be tactful and understanding when you check them and feed the mare.

Catching the foal (Fig. 2)
To catch the foal, a knowledgeable assistant will be necessary, because the foal will probably slip away to the far side of his dam. With the mare and foal in a stable, make use of the wall. If the assistant stands at the mare's head, blocking the line of escape between the mare and the wall, it will be possible for you to approach the foal quietly from behind and take it between your arms, one arm round the chest, the other round the quarters. It is essential that the foal is not allowed to get away from you. After a few days the foal will relax while you are holding him in this way and can be rubbed on the neck and gradually along the back and loins, round the base of the ears and down the nose, to prepare him for fitting a foal slip.

Fitting a foal slip (Fig. 3)
A Dutch foal slip is the easiest to fit and is less rigid on the head. Preferably it should be made of soft, supple leather, to minimise any likelihood of chafing or cutting the foal's tender skin. It must fit correctly, being neither too loose nor too tight.

With both the headpiece and the noseband unbuckled, slip the strap of the headpiece over the foal's neck, fasten it and then move it up to its correct position behind the ears. Place the noseband strap in the flat of your hand and quietly slip it over the nose, then fasten it.

In the confines of the stable, allow the foal time to accept the strange feeling of the leather round his head. Foals grow so quickly that this fit must be checked every day.

Foals

Fig. 3 A Dutch foal slip
correctly fitted.

Leading in hand (Fig. 4)
The first lesson should take place in the stable or in a very
safe confined area, with an assistant to lead the mare.
Although the foal may have a foal slip on, at this stage it
must not be used to hold or lead him.

The safe way to hold the foal is by making use of a stable
rubber. Folded diagonally and placed round his neck, it can
be held in one hand, by the withers. The other hand should be
placed round his quarters. (Fig. 4).

Fig. 4 A safe way to lead the foal.

The mare should be led a few steps at a time by an assistant while the foal is held and encouraged to move forward and follow her. This is the groundwork for leading in hand. The foal will begin to learn the commands 'Walk on' and 'Stand'.

It is most important in these very early lessons during the first few days, that the foal does not get away from you.

Turning out the mare and foal
If the mare has been stabled for foaling, she and her foal should be taken out into the fresh air after twenty-four hours, as long as the weather is reasonably dry.

A safe, well-fenced field is necessary. Wire is dangerous and even small lengths of it must be made obvious by the use of strips of plastic or fabric. All gates on the way to the field must be open in readiness.

When turning the mare and foal out for the first time it is sensible to have three people: two to control the foal and one to lead the mare. The mare will normally be led out first. The assistant leading her must be mindful of any problems which might occur with the foal behind her. If necessary, the mare must wait for the foal until both are reassured of the other's presence before proceeding. The foal will usually follow, being cradled and controlled by an assistant on each side. If the mare is reluctant to leave the stable, the foal may be taken out first. If the foal is reluctant, it may be better to ease him out backwards in front of the mare.

Once out of the stable the foal should be guided to walk fairly close to his mother. It could be dangerous to allow him to follow loose. On entering the field and having shut the gate, it is sensible to lead the pair round to accustom them to the boundaries, to help calm them down and to check that the foal is following his mother naturally while under the control of the handlers. Before letting them loose, it is important to go well into the centre of the field, bring the foal round in front of the mare, and release them both together.

If you are bringing the mare and foal in at night you will need three people to work together in the same way as when turning them out. First catch the mare and lead her to the edge of the field by a safe fence or hedge. You can then use this barrier in the same way that you used the stable wall to catch the foal (Figs. 2 and 5).

Further lessons in leading
During the next stage in 'leading', a rope may be threaded through the back ring of the foal slip (*never clipped on*) and used in conjunction with the stable rubber to control the foal. As he becomes more obedient, the rope will replace the stable rubber as a means of control, but it is still better to check forward-rushes by putting your arm round his chest rather than by using the foal slip, which could cause pressure on the poll region, or make him fall in an unnatural way. Either of these could cause permanent damage. Encouragement to move forward must come from your hand behind his quarters. If something goes wrong, keep one end of the rope in your hand, and allow the foal to slip free. A loose foal with a flapping rope will panic.

Fig. 5 Helping the foal to return to the stable.

Once the foal has learned to walk confidently 'in hand' in a foal slip and rope, you may extend the education. Walk the foal round the mare, who is held by an assistant. Walk away and back. Eventually you will be able to trot him back, always continuing on past the mare to establish discipline. The foal will now have the word 'Ter-rot' added to his vocabulary.

Stable manners (also handling for grooming, veterinary attention and the farrier)
In the first few days, the foal will have been caught, taught to stand and to be handled. This must now extend to accepting being stroked and rubbed all over his body, gradually working down the legs. Each leg in turn may be picked up just off the ground for a very short time. The foal will begin to comprehend 'Hold up'.

Handling is very important, as you may need to control the foal well enough to wash and dry his hindquarters if he scours. (See page 23.)

General handling will progress towards grooming and picking out feet, so that the foal is confident when visited by the farrier and the veterinary surgeon.

From the beginning, insist on good behaviour. The foal must be confident but at the same time must respect you. He should be taught good stable manners from an early age.

An introduction to tying up
Initially when groomed, the foal may be held by an assistant with a rope threaded through the foal slip. The next stage is to thread a longer rope through a suitable wall ring, and hold that in one hand while grooming with the other.

The foal must be made to 'Stand'. Any pulling back must be discouraged immediately by a scold and insistence that the foal moves forward, if necessary with a slap on the quarters. This is as far as one need go with this training until the mare and foal are being given concentrated feeds towards the end of the summer.

Initially the foal may nibble from the mare's bowl on the ground, but if she is jealous over her feed, care must be taken. Once the taste is established, the foal can be taught to use his own manger, well off the ground, so that he can feed comfortably and not feel disadvantaged.

Eventually, when the foal eats happily and has learned to accept the restriction of a rope, the mare and foal may be tied up while feeding. Do not go out of earshot and, as always, tie up to a loop of breakable string attached to the wall ring.

Never leave a foal alone with nothing to do when tied up. He might make a bid to escape – undoing all your good work, and injuring himself in the process.

Teaching a foal to be worldly
While the foal is under the reassuring influence of his mother it is advantageous to let him become accustomed to the sights and sounds of the farm. If possible, turn the mare and foal out in a field next to a road, so that he learns to accept traffic. Horse shows are best avoided unless you are confident that you will have control, and have an experienced person to help you.

Travel
The mare and foal may need to travel – for example, when they return from the stud where the foal was born. Transporting the foal will be easier if the mare is 100% reliable herself. Loading rarely presents problems, but pre-planning is important. Make safe any gaps between the ramp and the floor of the box to prevent the foal's tiny hooves from getting caught up. Three people will be needed: one to lead the mare and one on each side of the foal. If the mare is the slightest bit doubtful, load the foal first, closely followed by the mare. Alternatively, take the mare up slowly, with the foal helped up close behind. Handle the foal as shown in Fig. 5.

Mare and foal should travel together loose and should have plenty of space. For this reason, trailers may not be suitable.

Unloading needs even more care. Choose a quiet, confined area, and if possible handle the foal on to and down the ramp first. The mare will follow. If this is difficult, the mare, and the foal following her, must be kept close together. Do not allow a foal to come down a ramp by himself.

Weaning

The separation of mare and foal is a traumatic experience for both of them. Generally, foals are weaned at six months, but this depends on the condition of the mare and the foal, on weather conditions, and on your plans for the mare. If the mare is not required for riding, and is not in foal again, it is beneficial for the growth of the foal to leave him with the mare until the following spring, provided the mare is fed accordingly through the winter. Conversely, a yearling who has not been weaned will be strong, mentally more independent and possibly more difficult to handle.

The foal must be used to eating concentrates before he is weaned so that his digestive system can cope with the ultimate change of diet.

The kindest way to wean is to separate two mares and foals who have been turned out together. You will need a competent assistant. The mares should be taken a considerable distance from the foals, certainly out of earshot and preferably to another establishment. The separation is best made a little before dusk, so that the darkness of night helps to calm down both mares and foals.

Put the two foals together in a well-bedded loosebox. At first the top door to the stable must be shut because they will try to return to their mothers. They will be distressed for a while, sometimes sweating and digging up the bed.

The mares should be quickly taken away to avoid any further distress. They should be be turned out in a distant, secure field. They will fret and neigh for their foals, but will soon settle down. Their feeds should be reduced considerably for about a week, during which time the milk should dry up. Watch the udders, and, if they become swollen and tender consult the vet.

The foals should be kept shut up for two or three days. Then you can turn them out in a well-fenced field. It is necessary to keep a foal separated from its mother for at least six weeks to complete the weaning. It is during this time, when the foal is most dependent on you, that you must establish a closer relationship, and his education in handling, grooming and leading should progress.

If you are unable to arrange for a second mare and foal to wean with yours, the foal will best settle with a gentle companion in a stable which is familiar.

Veterinary attention
It is important to seek veterinary advice on the foal's immunisation and worming programme. As long as the mare has been immunised against tetanus and influenza at the proper intervals, the antibodies in her milk will give the foal adequate protection for some time.

The foal's worming programme should start at about six weeks, and his own immunisation programme against tetanus and influenza at about six months.

The time chosen to geld a colt depends on growth, development and behaviour. Your veterinary surgeon will be the best judge.

5

Yearlings, Two- and Three-Year-Olds

Yearlings

General Care

Yearlings should be given every facility to develop naturally and steadily, both in body growth and mental ability. Attention must be given to their general condition. Unbalanced feeding or undue stress on the limbs can cause problems in the development of bones and joints. Regular visits from the farrier will ensure that the feet grow correctly.

Youngstock are particularly vulnerable to worm infestation. Worm damage at this age can result in serious, though often hidden, weakness for life, affecting general health or causing an unexpected disaster to an apparently fit, mature horse. Consult your veterinary surgeon, who will have up-to-date knowledge of the preparations available.

Young, growing animals need the freedom of living out naturally, but it is necessary to provide protection from flies in the summer. In the winter they should be brought in at night, as access to shelter and a deep, dry bed will enable them to obtain maximum benefit from the food given. This combined system also ensures that they are handled regularly.

Physiology
All youngstock should appear healthy and alert. Yearlings will still be growing rapidly, and as they develop they may look gawky and unfurnished. Their manes and tails will be changing from fluffy, foal quality, to adult hair, and will be short and untidy.

Psychology
Yearlings, especially colts, can be very naughty, and are still curious, playful and erratic in their behaviour. They are becoming more assertive and are strong enough to take advantage of you unless you are alert. Mentally, you must be one jump ahead of them, so that, without being tense, you can anticipate what might happen if they suddenly make unexpected moves. Paying due attention to the safety of your equipment, the environment and the way you handle your youngster, will help you to avoid accidents.

Education
At this stage the yearling needs freedom to play. His concentration is limited and he is easily bored. However, some discipline is necessary. He must learn to walk alongside you when being led – neither barging forward nor hanging back.

While you are leading him, it is prudent to wear a hard hat, gloves and sensible footwear.

New experiences will be encountered while he is being led between the stable and the field or during short walks away from home. Remember to handle and lead from both the left- and right-hand side. If you are carrying a whip, hold it in your outside hand. It can be used behind your back to ensure that he walks forward on command.

At home it may be acceptable to lead using a headcollar and rope. If you are in any doubt as to your ability to control the youngster, use a lungeing cavesson with a lungeing line or long rope attached to the centre ring. This will give you extra control, which is essential if you leave the safety of your own premises. A bit should not be used. To fit the lungeing cavesson. (See page 56.)

The nose is a very tender part of the horse, so the youngster will learn quickly to respect and pay attention to the restraining aid through the cavesson. While always maintaining the upper hand, do not abuse the advantage that the cavesson will give you, or you could lose some sensitivity for the future, or even damage the delicate cartilage of the yearling's nose. If he now begins to learn that a 'take and give' or a quick vibration means 'Steady' and 'Halt' (used in conjunction with your voice), an important line of communication will have been opened. In years to come, this will follow through as the contact with the hand develops when he is lunged, and will later be in the form of the contact between your hand and his mouth when he is ridden.

Every time that he is handled in the stable, the yearling should be tied up and should accept it without question. The elementary handling which began during his foal days should be continued with some basic grooming, picking out the feet and insisting on good stable manners.

Two-Year-Olds

General care
As for yearlings.

Physiology
Two-year-olds are still very immature. Their growth rate will have slowed down, but the bones are still developing and the muscles are beginning to take form.

Yearlings, Two- and Three-Year-Olds

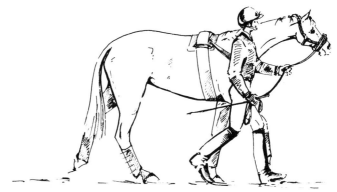

Leading the two-year-old from the 'off' side.

Psychology

The same problems exist with two-year-olds as with year-lings, but if they have been handled well they should be more sensible and obedient.

Colts should have been gelded by the April of their two-year-old year. Uncut colts of this age will be fertile, by nature dominant, and even aggressive. They will require especially careful handling. Fillies can be flighty and silly, especially when in season.

Education

Leading in hand should be continued, and education should be broadened by introducing new sights and sounds in a safe environment. Use the commands through the leading rein and voice, as suggested for the yearling. Remember to lead and handle from either side.

The two-year-old should accept handling and being brushed on his head, body and legs. Late in the year, rollers, rugs and boots may be introduced. It is important to introduce new equipment in a way which does not frighten your youngster. Extra time and trouble taken initially will help to produce a level-headed, confident horse, whereas bad experiences at this stage may cause apprehension and fear of anything new for many years to come. Allow time for the youngster to see, smell and hear the noise that a new item may make before proceeding further. His own stable is the best place to introduce new equipment.

Rollers (Fig. 6)
Before introducing any rug, the two-year-old should be accustomed to the feel of a roller. Many horses will be upset by this unusual restriction, and their natural reaction may be to try to get rid of it by bucking. This can be avoided by careful planning.

Before fitting the roller, some people pass an elasticated tail bandage round the girth area and secure it with an easily released half-bow. During this initiation an assistant will be needed to hold and reassure the horse.

When the horse has accepted the feel of the bandage for short periods, a padded web roller can be introduced. Use a pad to ensure that there is no undue pressure on the backbone. It must be secured to the roller to prevent it from slipping. At first the roller should not be fastened too tightly, so to stop it slipping back a breast girth must be fitted. A practical way of doing this is to organise a loop at the end of the breast girth, through which the strap of the roller can be passed. Then proceed as follows:

1. With an assistant holding and reassuring the horse, show him the roller. It should be folded to prevent it flapping against him.
2. Stroke him with the roller on his neck, shoulders and back.
3. If he is relaxed, move the roller into position, with the pad under it, and stroke his back with it a few more times; also stroke him with your hand all the way under his belly.
4. Gently unfold the roller so that it moves down his off side, and with one hand holding it on his back, reach down with the other and take hold of the end. Pass it through the loop of the breast girth (which can be handed to you by an assistant) and buckle it up loosely.

5. Wait for a moment and tighten the roller, one hole at a time. Move the horse one or two steps between each tightening. Soon the roller will be tight enough to stay in place. It must not be over-restrictive.

Meanwhile, you and your assistant should continually reassure the horse with hand and voice, remembering that he may suddenly take exception to the feel of the roller, and leap forward.

After several sessions, and once the horse is more relaxed, he may be left loose in his stable for a short time with the roller and breast girth in place.

Teaching the young horse to accept the roller is an essential preliminary to fitting a rug and later a saddle.

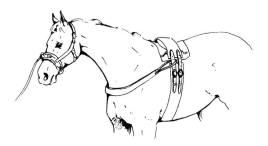

Fig. 6 The roller correctly fitted; showing the loop on the breast girth.

Rugs
The initial introduction of a rug is best made with a large towel or a piece of blanket which can be slipped on and off easily with one hand. An assistant should hold the horse for you. First, allow the youngster to examine the blanket, then run your hands firmly along his back from withers to quarters. Concertina the blanket and then place it well forward over the withers. When he is standing calmly, pull it out gently over the back with one hand. Allow it to stay in place for a few moments, while reassuring him.

To remove the blanket the first few times, slide back the front edge to join the back edge, and lift it off carefully. Stroking him over the quarters with your hand will prepare him for removing the blanket by sliding it over his tail. Before long, you will be able to put on and take off the blanket in the usual way. When he has learned this lesson, a full-size rug may be introduced.

The rug, folded in half, must also be shown to the horse before it is quietly placed over the withers. When accepted, unfold it back over the quarters until it is correctly in place, and leave it unbuckled. After this stage, as long as he is relaxed, fasten the front of the rug and fit the roller and breast girth as described above.

Fig. 7 Introducing the blanket.

New Zealand rugs. Allow the horse to smell the rug and to listen to the sound that the stiff material can make. When this is accepted – but before you fit the rug – run your hands over his back and body, down his quarters and around his hind legs where the straps will be. Stand in a safe position. Fit the rug in the stable and allow time for the horse to move about and accept the rug before turning him out.

Rugs with cross-under straps, correctly adjusted, stay in place efficiently and comfortably, and avoid any risk of damage to the back. In most cases they are preferable to a rug and roller, but the feel of the roller is a useful introduction to the use of the girth.

Rugs with a fixed surcingle can bring pressure to bear on the spine and are not recommended.

All rugs should be correctly shaped, because they will stay in place and be more comfortable for the horse.

Boots
Sooner or later the horse must become accustomed to wearing boots or bandages around his legs. If the youngster is shod, he must become used to wearing boots before lungeing lessons can begin. The most useful type are lightweight brushing boots with Velcro fastenings.

After showing him the boots and accustoming him to the sound of the Velcro, stroke him down the legs with the boot. When this is accepted you can fasten the boot in position, securing the middle strap first. Both front boots should be fitted and the youngster should be moved round the stable with them on. The same procedure should then be followed with the hind legs, when it is more likely that a reaction will occur. Many youngsters, feeling the boots for the first time will pick up their legs very high and may kick out, but after a few exaggerated steps they normally settle down. Bulky travelling boots should not be used for this initiation.

Lungeing
Well-developed two-year-olds may be taught to lunge towards the end of this year, but it is not generally advisable to begin until they are three years old. Before attempting to lunge your youngster please read *Lungeing* (Chapter 6).

Three-Year-Olds

General care and physiology
The appearance of three-year-olds is deceptive. They often look far more mature than they are, and it may be tempting

The three-year-old becoming familiar with his saddlery.

to work them too hard. During the year, handling and leading will progress to lungeing and backing, but remember that the bones are still soft and that too much work can cause defects and can stunt growth.

While the teeth are changing, the mouth may be very tender. It may be sensible to curtail lessons, especially those which involve wearing a bit.

At 2½ years the front milk teeth drop out, and the permanent teeth begin to grow into place. This takes about six months.

At 3½ years the laterals change.

At 4½ years the corners change.

Psychology

The well-handled three-year-old should mentally be self-confident and relaxed. He should be ready to complete the part of his education which will result in him carrying a rider. Take care not to over-do a lesson and tire the youngster mentally or physically. The experienced trainer will know how long each session should last. Fatigue or boredom may result in resistance, but the lesson should end on a good note, even if this takes a little longer than anticipated, and demands patient perseverance from the trainer.

Education

As always, several aspects of the horse's education will overlap, and revision is important to confirm previous lessons. A well-handled three-year-old should accept being tied up, but steps should still be taken to prevent him from running back and frightening or injuring himself. Tie him up during grooming, and for all stable duties, and continue to insist on good stable manners.

General handling should include stroking him all over his body and gently slapping him on both sides of his neck, shoulders, back and rump. He will learn to be saddled from either side and will accept the noise and feel of the saddle being slapped. He must have confidence in the people who handle him, so if he becomes tense, he must be reassured patiently, and allowed to relax before any more new ground is covered.

If, as suggested, boots have been introduced during the previous year, the horse should accept their fitting as a matter of course, and should wear them when being led about in the lungeing cavesson.

He will be familiar with his immediate surroundings, such as the yard, the schooling area and the field. He will have walked past cars and heavier vehicles parked in the yard, and will probably have watched traffic on the road from a safe distance. His first step towards jumping will be taken when he meets a pole or small log on the ground, examines it, and walks over it while he is being led.

It is usual to introduce the bridle and saddle during the three-year-old year.

Bridles

Initially it is easier if the bit is attached to the sliphead of a double bridle, as it can simply be fitted over the ears, and the height of the bit can be adjusted with one buckle. Bearing in mind the size and shape of the horse's mouth, choose a mild, lightweight snaffle which will fit and suit him. Adjust the sliphead to a generous length, fit it *over* the headcollar, then raise the bit into the correct position. You will have practised gently opening the horse's mouth and handling his ears during previous lessons. Once he is accustomed to this, putting on the bridle should present no problem (Fig. 8).

For the first day or so, remove the sliphead or bridle after a few minutes, as the mouth will be sensitive. Lower the bit slowly and allow it to drop out of his mouth gently, without banging against his teeth.

Fig. 8 Gently opening his mouth.

Later, the horse can be led out or lunged, wearing his cavesson and bridle. Control should be from the cavesson. No siderein or lungeing line should be attached to the bit. During this time the horse will become confident with the feel of the bit and should learn to hold it softly in his mouth.

Saddles

At first a small, light saddle, without stirrups, should be used. A soft, synthetic girth is preferable to a cold leather one, and a breast girth is essential. Introduce the saddle, and then fit it in the same way as the roller (see page 47). Do not allow the girth to swing or frighten the horse. Lead the horse round the stable with the saddle and breast girth fitted, but do not leave him alone in the stable, because he may try to rub it off or roll on it.

Lungeing

Before he is backed, the horse should be working happily and obediently on the lunge, wearing a saddle and bridle. See the following chapter.

6

Lungeing

Before you can teach a young horse to lunge you must be able to control an experienced horse on the lunge. It is important for you to understand the difference between good and bad lungeing, and to know what your aims should be. You will need plenty of practice, first lungeing a quiet, educated horse and later a variety of horses. Only experience will give you the confidence and skill needed to lunge a young or previously unlunged horse.

The purposes of lungeing are:
□ To exercise a horse.
□ To train the young horse.
□ To retrain, improve or supple an older horse.
□ To train riders. (This is fully explained in the Pony Club *Instructor's Handbook*.)

Equipment
A simple snaffle bridle with the noseband and reins removed. (Bridles are not necessary for the young horse's early lessons.) A bridle with reins should be used when lungeing a rider.

Lungeing

A *lungeing cavesson* (Fig. 9). There are several different patterns available. The noseband should be well padded. Generally there are three rings on a hinged metal plate attached to the front of it. Some types are designed to be fitted under the bit (e.g. a drop noseband), or above the bit (e.g. a cavesson noseband). Most lungeing cavessons are fitted with the noseband in the higher position. A jowl strap must be fitted firmly around the cheek bones of the horse so that the cheekpieces cannot pull forward and touch the horse's eye.

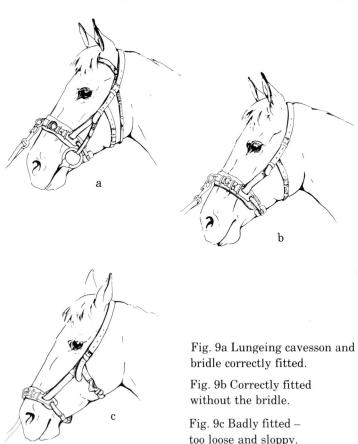

Fig. 9a Lungeing cavesson and bridle correctly fitted.

Fig. 9b Correctly fitted without the bridle.

Fig. 9c Badly fitted – too loose and sloppy.

The noseband must also be fastened snugly. If a bridle is used, the lungeing cavesson should be fitted over it, but the jowl strap and noseband may be fitted either under or over the cheekpiece of the bridle: whichever is more comfortable for the horse.

If there is any doubt about the correct fitting of the lungeing cavesson, expert advice should be sought, for a horse will remember and associate discomfort or pain with his exercise far more readily than he will recall praise or pleasure. If he is uncomfortable, he will dislike work and will learn to evade it.

A lunge line should be made of webbing, lampwick or rope. Nylon cannot be recommended. It will never break, can cut and burn, and is therefore dangerous. The line should be approximately 24–30 ft (8–10 m) long, and should be fastened to the centre ring of the cavesson.

A lungeing roller or a correctly fitted saddle may be used. A breast girth or breast-plate should always be used on a young horse to prevent the roller or saddle from slipping back. If the roller or saddle slips too far forward, a crupper will be needed. (Seek expert advice to fit it.) The roller should have two Ds on either side. The saddle should have its stirrups removed or firmly fastened up (Fig. 10).

A lungeing whip should be light and with a good length of thong. It should feel well balanced and comfortable to handle.

Side reins should be made of leather and not too heavy. They should be about 5–6 ft (1.5–1.8 m) in length, with a buckle and strap at one end and a clip at the other. Some have an elastic or rubber insert. The buckle end is fitted under the saddle flaps to the girth straps (Fig. 11) and the clip attached to the bit or cavesson side-rings. The side reins should not be clipped on until the horse is in the lungeing area, but they should be adjusted ready for use. They should be of equal length and long enough to be just in contact when the horse is standing in balance. When they are not attached to the bit or cavesson, they should be secured – ideally by each being

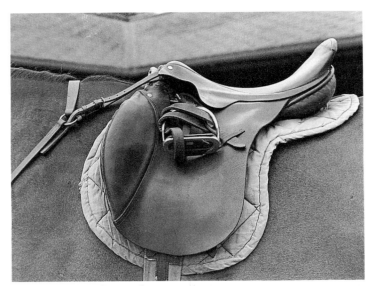

Fig. 10 Stirrups fastened up.

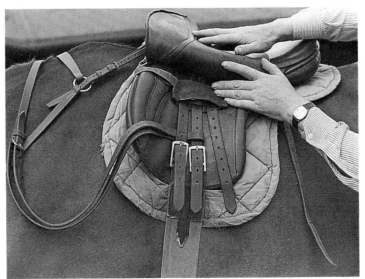

Fig. 11 Side reins fitted to the girth straps.

passed over the withers and clipped to the D on the opposite side of the saddle or roller.

(Side reins will not be needed for the young horse's early lessons.)

Fore and hind brushing boots should be fitted to the horse for protection. If the horse is unshod, the fitting of brushing boots is recommended but not essential.

The lunger must wear sensible clothes, suitable footwear, gloves and a hard hat. Spurs must not be worn.

Principles

The lunger must give his full concentration to the horse, and must speak only to him. Good lungeing will teach obedience, improve the balance, rhythm and paces of the horse, and aid correct muscular development. Bad lungeing will provoke tension, disobedience, unbalanced carriage and irregular paces.

The lunger must be quiet, patient and confident, and encourage his horse to become calm and relaxed. If the horse is upset he will lose his concentration, balance and co-ordination, and may easily slip and fall.

Aims

☐ The lunger should maintain a steady contact with the horse through the lunge line, and should work the horse on a true circle, trying to keep his position in the centre.

☐ The paces should be steady, regular and energetic, but not hurried.

☐ The horse should lunge equally well on both reins, appearing to bend uniformly from poll to tail on the line of the circle (Fig. 12).

☐ Once the horse has reached the stage when he is wearing a bridle and side reins, he should always seek the contact of the bit. Since he will be moving on a circle, contact will be made

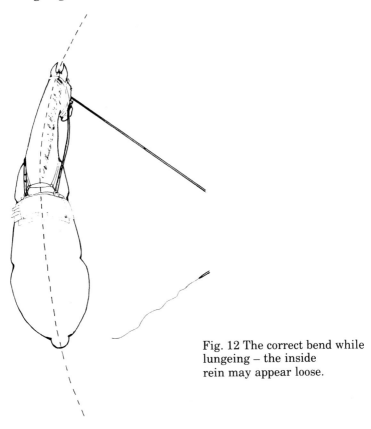

Fig. 12 The correct bend while
lungeing – the inside
rein may appear loose.

with the outside rein. When this is achieved, the inside rein
may appear loose.

☐ The outline of the horse should relate to his level of training and maturity (Fig. 13).

If the lungeing is satisfactory, the very young horse will start
by having a very long, low, outline which will gradually
appear 'rounder'. As his hind legs become more engaged, and
his back more supple, he will take more weight with his hind
legs and will become lighter on his forehand. His neck will

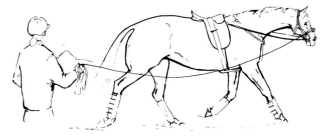

Fig. 13a The very long, low outline.

Fig. 13b The hind-quarters becoming more engaged – a slightly more advanced outline.

then become more arched and his head more raised. This gradual improvement will take place over a long period of time, as the appropriate muscles develop; it will only happen if the horse is being worked correctly.

Control
The horse should have respect for and confidence in his trainer and:
☐ Become obedient to voice commands.
☐ Respond to the restraining aid of the lunge line (a 'take and give' or a quick vibration).
☐ Respect and accept – but not fear – the whip, moving freely forward when it is directed to his quarters or moving on to a larger circle when it is pointed towards the girth. It may not be necessary for the whip thong to touch the horse (Fig. 14).

61

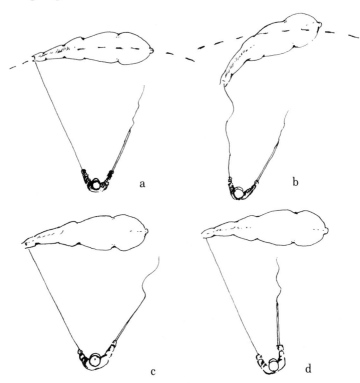

Fig. 14a The correct position for lungeing.

Fig. 14b The lunger too far forward – the horse can 'turn in'.

Fig. 14c Asking the horse to move freely forward.

Fig. 14d Asking the horse to move onto a larger circle or for more bend.

Lungeing area

An indoor school or outdoor arena is ideal. The corner of a well-drained level field is adequate. All exits should be closed. Horses must never be lunged on a slippery or unlevel surface.

It is advisable to lunge a young horse in an enclosed space, within the lungeing area, even if this means erecting make-shift barriers, such as barrels and poles. A minimum space of 20 m×20 m is required; 20 m×40 m is ideal as this allows the lunger space to vary the site of his circle and not make a 'track'.

Position of the lunger (Fig. 14)
The lunger should stand in a balanced, upright position. He should face the horse's girth, but should watch the whole horse. His body should turn in the direction in which the horse is moving and should never be in front of the horse's shoulder.

When the horse is on the left rein, the whip should be in the right hand and the tip should be raised and pointing towards the ribs or the quarters of the horse as desired. Ideally the lunger should be able to maintain his position in the centre of the circle.

With young untrained or stiff horses, he may walk a small circle, almost following the horse but being central enough to avoid a kick.

Holding the lunge line (Fig. 15)
The excess lunge line should be folded in loops and held in the palm of the one hand, with the forearm in a line to the horse's

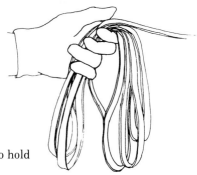

Fig. 15 A good way to hold the lunge line.

Lungeing

mouth. The elbow allows a forward and backward movement, thereby maintaining a steady contact. Some people prefer to hold the excess lunge line in the other hand so that both hands can be used on the lunge line if extra strength is required. It is appropriate to use this method when lungeing a young horse. Never wrap the lunge line around the hand.

The voice
The horse recognises the note and tone of the voice as well as the actual words. It is important for the lunger always to use the same tones and words. Transitions up should always have a rising note, and transitions down a falling one. Transitions up may be supported by a movement of the whip. The young horse will already recognise words that he has been taught while being led. Continuity should be maintained.

Use the voice sparingly. Some suggested commands are:

Transitions up
'WALK ON'. The voice starts low and rises at the end.
'TERR-ROT'. As above.
'CAN-TER'. As above.

Transitions down
'AND TERR-ROT'. The note of the voice drops from a high note to a lower one.
'AND WALK'. As above.
'HALT'. As above and rather drawn out.

Other commands
'STEADY'. A very even tone.
'GOOD'. Voice calm, steady, but encouraging.
'WALK', 'TROT', or 'CANTER ON'. The word 'ON' used briskly but eagerly, for increased impulsion.

Method with a previously lunged horse
The horse should be tacked up in the stable, using the equipment and fitting methods already described. The side reins should not be clipped to the bit until lungeing has begun.

The lunger, if leading from the near-side, should have the carefully folded lunge line in his left hand and lead with his right hand placed sufficiently close to the cavesson to have adequate control. The whip, with thong secured, should be held under the left arm or in the left hand, the tip facing backwards (Fig. 16). In principle, the whip should never be put down on the ground.

On reaching the prepared area, the lunger should halt the horse, check both sides, and while speaking calmly, introduce the horse to the whip, so that he is not alarmed.

Fig. 16 Leading the horse into the lungeing area.

Near the centre of what will become the lungeing circle, the lunger stands facing the horse's girth and steps back, carefully playing out some of the line so that the horse's head is not pulled inwards, and asking the horse with voice and directed whip to 'Walk on'. Making sure that he stays behind the line of the horse's shoulder, the lunger must send the horse forward and out on to an expanding circle by pointing the whip, with a light upwards motion, towards the girth, at the same time allowing the lunge line to be played out.

When walking calmly on the circle, the horse is asked to trot. Once he is settled, and gets any joyful behaviour out of his system, the lunger may bring him back to halt through walk. He should halt and wait, without turning in.

The lunger should speak kindly, tuck the whip (pointing backwards) under his arm, and approach the horse's shoulder. The lunge line should be carefully folded as the lunger walks towards the horse.

The side reins may now be attached to the bit. They should be of equal length and must not restrict the horse's head and neck. As a rough guide they should be just in contact when the horse is standing in balance; once he is trotting they may appear loose.

As the horse works he should stretch forward and down and seek the contact of the side reins (Fig. 13). This is one of the most important requirements of good lungeing. As the horse bends correctly on the curve of the circle, the inside side rein may appear slightly loose (Fig. 12).

It is far better to have the side reins too loose than too tight. When the horse has begun to find his balance and to work correctly, a steady but energetic rhythm should result as he stretches forward and down to seek the bit.

After five minutes or so on one rein, the horse should be brought to a halt. The side reins should be unclipped from the bit and secured to the Ds, as described. The horse should be allowed a brief period of relaxation, after which he should be led through the centre of the circle. Then the side reins should be refitted and lungeing started on the other rein. Equal time should be spent on both reins. During sustained periods of walk, and while changing the rein, the side reins should be unfastened and secured to the saddle or roller as before.

If the horse is persistently disobedient to the voice command to halt, aim him directly towards the perimeter wall of your lungeing area (as long as it is unjumpable). Direct him accurately, keeping him between the whip and rein to prevent him from turning when he reaches the wall. He will then be forced to halt. When he does, walk up to him and reward him with a pat and a kind word.

The content of the lungeing programme will be determined by the reason for lungeing and individual circumstances. Normally most of the work will be done at trot, but some short periods of walk should be included.

The fit horse may be lunged for a maximum of 20 to 30 minutes, with several changes of direction. The session should finish with a few minutes of free walk during which the horse should cool down before being returned to his stable.

During lungeing, constant attention must be paid to the horse, in order to establish his rhythm and balance. Unless he moves with supple regularity – his tail and back swinging, his steps unhurried but energetic – little of value will be accomplished.

The lunger will seek to achieve his objective with a combination of voice, whip and lunge line.

Good lungeing is like riding the horse, but from the ground.

Before teaching a horse to lunge
If you can control an experienced horse on the lunge, can understand the principles of good lungeing, and know what

Lungeing

you are hoping to achieve, you should be able to train a young
horse (or an older but previously unlunged horse) to lunge. It
is sensible to gain experience by teaching a pony or a more
placid horse to lunge before attempting to teach a lively
youngster. Unless you are very experienced, it is essential to
have an assistant.

When to begin. It is useful, at any stage of training, for an
older horse to know how to be lunged. Young horses are
generally started at three-years old, but big strong horses or
ponies may begin training on the lunge as two-year-olds.
Weak or backward animals must be given more time to
mature.

Preliminaries. The horse must be familiar with wearing the
following equipment:
☐ A lungeing cavesson.
☐ A body roller or saddle.
☐ A breast-plate or breast girth.
☐ Brushing boots.
Use the methods described in Chapters 5 and 6 to introduce
and fit this equipment.

The horse must remember his earlier leading lessons and
must be obedient to the voice commands while being led from
a rope or short lunge line attached to the centre ring of the
cavesson. The commands for 'Slow down' and 'Halt' will be
given in conjunction with a quick 'take and give' of the lunge
line or rope. An ordinary schooling whip should be carried in
the outside hand, and should be aimed towards his flank to
make sure that he walks forward on the command. This will
serve as an introduction to the lungeing whip. The horse
should be led from either side and turn in either direction.

Method while training the horse to lunge
It is best to begin in the direction which is easiest for the
horse. Most are more comfortable working to the left.

To lunge the horse to the left, the trainer asks his assistant to stand by the horse's left shoulder, behind the lunge line, facing forward. It is preferable to have a very short piece of rope threaded through the inside ring of the cavesson, for the assistant to hold (Fig. 17).

The trainer says 'Walk on', while at the same time pointing the whip towards the horse's hindquarters, indicating that he should go forward. The assistant leads the horse forward and on to the lungeing circle, to help him to understand the trainer's wishes. Later on, when the horse understands and walks willingly forward, the assistant removes the rope from the cavesson and simply walks beside the horse to prevent him from turning in and losing the contact of the lunge line. This contact should be maintained in as unvarying a way as possible, in the same way as a rider should maintain contact through the rein.

At all times the trainer should be behind the horse's shoulder and should feel that he is almost driving the horse forward.

Occasionally, if a horse has a tendency to stop, suddenly swing away, or run back quickly, it may be better to position the assistant on the far side of the horse.

There are obvious advantages and disadvantages to both positions. If the assistant is on the inside, he could become entangled with the lunge line should the horse swing out-

Fig. 17 Teaching the horse to lunge.

wards or run back quickly. If he is on the outside, the horse could jump sideways on to him. However, if the assistant is on the outside, it is easier for him to 'fade away' when the trainer feels that he is ready to dispense with his services. The best solution will depend on the given circumstances at any particular time.

The trainer should speak directly to the horse and should use the assistant as a 'silent' helper to reassure the horse as necessary, and to enforce the commands which, at first, will be 'Walk on', 'Halt' and 'Walk on'. The horse must halt on the track without turning in to face the trainer.

The horse will soon understand that the 'take and give', or a quick vibration, has the same meaning when he is on the lunge as when he is being led, especially as it is used with the same voice commands.

The nose is a very sensitive part of the horse. The lunger, with the help of the assistant must establish and maintain obedience, but it should be remembered that considerable pain can be inflicted by violent jerking of the lunge line.

After practising 'Walk on' and 'Halt' a few times on each rein, the first lesson will be complete, and the horse can be put away. Lessons should not last longer than twenty minutes. After a few days it may be possible to manage without the assistant, though it is far better to ask him to return if problems arise.

When the horse is consistently calm and obedient in walk and halt, you can ask him to trot. At first there may be some difficulty over coming back to walk, but the trainer should remain calm and relaxed. Given time, the horse will tire, and walk of his own accord. As he does so, the trainer must be quick to use the right commands and praise him. It is only if fear and anxiety are introduced that real difficulties occur.

In cases of persistent disobedience, use the method of halting described on page 67.

Once the trot is established, side reins may be fastened to the side rings of the cavesson.

Future plans

If the youngster is only two-years old, lungeing should finish for the year as soon as he has become obedient, calm and sensible at walk and trot. In his three-year-old year, the same procedure should be adopted before new ground is covered.

Before he is backed, the horse must be lungeing fluently, wearing a saddle and bridle. By then he may be lunged in side reins attached to the bit. They should be adjusted to encourage a long, low outline. (See Fig. 13a.)

Canter should not be asked for in this early period of training, as it would over-excite the horse and put far too great a strain on his young limbs. However, before the ridden horse is cantered, it is sensible to achieve a few strides on the lunge, remembering the following:
☐ Side reins should not be used.
☐ Cantering should be very brief.
☐ It should be done on a large circle.
☐ It should be done in both directions.

7

Backing

Backing is part of the training procedure which teaches the young horse to accept a rider on his back.

Planning the time required for backing
Until now, work will probably have been intermittent: the young horse being worked for a few days at a time and then being left for a week or so. But once you decide that the time is right and that the horse is mature enough for backing, work should be on a daily basis until he has been backed and 'ridden away'. A skilled trainer with a well-handled horse may take about three weeks before backing, and may allow a further three or four weeks of regular work, to establish this part of his training.

Before beginning this stage, the horse must respect his handler and must be obedient. He must be lungeing fluently without being worried by his saddlery (Fig. 18).

Equipment
- ☐ Bridle.
- ☐ Saddle – use the saddle and bridle which the horse is being lunged in, with the addition of reins.
- ☐ Breast-plate.
- ☐ Lungeing cavesson and short lunge line.
- ☐ Neck strap – a stirrup leather buckled securely one-third of the way up the neck.
- ☐ Mounting block – a box or straw bale (which must not move and frighten the horse).
- ☐ Brushing boots.

When to back
Most horses are sufficiently developed to be backed in the autumn, as three-year-olds. They should then be given time to grow and develop for the rest of the winter.

If an immature horse is ridden too soon, permanent damage may be caused to limbs, back and attitude to work. However,

Fig. 18 Working fluently on the lunge before being backed.

it is sometimes advisable to back a big strong horse as a two-year-old before he becomes too powerful to be disciplined.

Some racehorses are backed towards the end of their second year, but they will have received specialised treatment and will be ridden only by lightweight riders.

It should be remembered that the bones and muscles are not sufficiently developed for the horse to work hard until he is at least five years old.

Where to back

Choose a familiar place where the horse feels safe and confident. Avoid wet and windy days.

For the first few times that the horse is backed, it is essential that there should be no outside disturbances which may unsettle or frighten him. If this happens and the horse moves suddenly, the rider may lose balance, frightening him still further. Such an experience may have lasting effects, and should be avoided at all costs. If the horse learns at this stage in his training that he can dislodge the rider he will try to use this again to his advantage.

An indoor school would seem to be an ideal place in which to back a horse, as long as the preliminaries to backing have taken place in that school. Alternatively, an outside arena may be used, or a sectioned-off corner of a well-fenced field where the horse is normally worked.

Some trainers use a large, high-roofed loosebox, as the horse may be more settled in his stable and less likely to object to the rider. There is, however, a danger of the rider being trapped if things should go wrong.

Preliminaries to backing

In the days or weeks before backing, the horse will be working on the lunge. At this time, steps should be taken to prepare him for the sounds and movements which will be made by his rider, and for the feeling of weight on his back.

He must also be introduced to the potentially threatening sight of the rider behind and above his eye level.

Much of this work will be introduced in the stable, while the horse is being tacked up, during grooming, or after work. Later, some of it will be in the area where the horse will be backed, during lungeing or leading sessions.

As the work progresses a lightweight rider will be needed. At later stages, some trainers use an assistant to leg-up and support the rider. All helpers should be quiet and tactful.

The trainer should be in command, because the horse will have learned to feel secure under his guidance. The horse will respond best to his trainer's voice, because it is familiar and meaningful to him. The rider will be able to work quietly round the horse while the trainer holds him and provides a calming influence.

Remember to work equally on each side of the horse and to reassure the horse with a quiet voice and a soothing hand.

Progressively, over a period of time, the horse should learn to accept in a confident way, the following preliminaries to backing:

☐ Being stroked and gently slapped on his neck, shoulders and back.
☐ The rider standing by his shoulder and carefully jumping up and down.
☐ Being lunged with the stirrup irons hanging down by his side. (The leathers must be short enough to prevent the stirrups from hitting the horse's elbows or from swinging back and bumping his ribs or flanks.)
☐ The rider standing on a straw bale placed by the horse's shoulder, so that the horse becomes accustomed to seeing his rider out of the corner of his eye. The rider can then reach over and pat the horse on the opposite side as well as the near-side (Fig. 19a).
☐ The rider standing on the straw bale, continuing to pat the

Backing

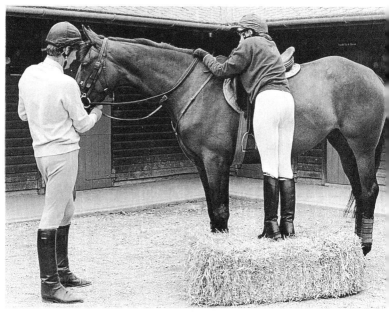

Fig. 19a Almost as high as a rider.

horse and then pressing down with his hand on the saddle.

☐ Carrying the weight of the rider. Having removed the stirrups, the trainer slowly legs up the rider, who leans across the front of the saddle, keeping still at first and then gently stroking and patting the horse. (An assistant may be needed to leg up and support the rider.) Some trainers prefer to progress from standing on the straw bale to leaning across the horse, but there is a danger that if the horse moves quickly, the bale might be in the way and become an extra hazard.

☐ Finally, when the horse is settled and has accepted the rider's weight, the trainer can ask him to move forward a step. The trainer or an assistant will support the rider. The rider then slips down. This is repeated until the horse is happy to carry the rider for several steps without becoming tense or worried (Figs. 19b and c).

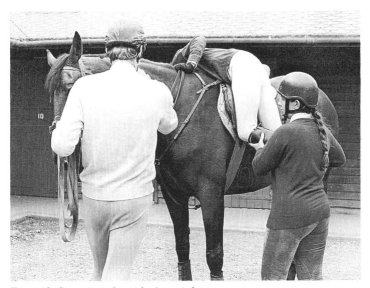

Fig. 19b Carrying the rider's weight.

Fig. 19c Patting the horse before slipping down.

Backing

If the horse becomes upset or frightened at any point during the above work, the trainer must return to the previous stage and proceed patiently and calmly until the horse regains confidence.

NB: The time taken for these preparatory stages depends on the temperament and outlook of the horse. Some will accept everything calmly after a few days, while others may take longer. The good trainer will have assessed the horse's attitude by noting how he reacted in various circumstances, and will progress accordingly.

Backing

In time, the horse will be ready for the rider to sit astride his back. This is best achieved on a day when the horse has been well settled on the lunge and is accepting the work in a calm and disciplined manner.

With the stirrups removed, the trainer legs up the rider, who begins by leaning over the horse, as described above. The rider then puts his right leg over the horse, being very careful not to touch his quarters, or the cantle of the saddle.

The rider does not sit up at first, but continues to lean forward. He should hold the neck strap for security with one hand and the reins very loosely with the other. The unusual sensations of feeling the weight and seeing the shape of the rider in an upright position at the same time could be of great concern to the horse (Fig. 20).

When the trainer is satisfied that the horse has accepted the rider's weight and legs by his sides, he can suggest that the rider sits up slowly. The look in the horse's eye, the way in which he moves his ears, and his breathing pattern are all signs which the trainer should take into account. The trainer should continually reassure the horse with his voice. A tense horse will hold his back muscles in a tight, tense manner (back up). The rider should be able to feel this and should therefore be able to tell when the horse is tense and when he is more relaxed and accepting the weight. The way in which the horse holds his tail is a helpful guide. If it is clamped down, the horse's back will be tense and he will need more time to relax.

Fig. 20 Accepting the rider's weight and the sight of his legs.

Before the horse is asked to walk on, the rider should gently shift in the saddle to prepare him for the extra unaccustomed movement. Once this is accepted, the trainer may ask for the first steps.

At this stage, the horse will not understand the rider's leg or hand aids. The rider's task is a passive one, simply to sit, in balance and without tension. The trainer should use the voice commands with which the horse is familiar. Asking him to walk on, he should lead him forward. The horse should then be halted and praised. Once he is relaxed, a few more steps may be taken. The way in which the horse reacts will determine how quickly progress can be made.

The stirrups may be introduced when the trainer feels that the horse is happy about the rider's legs hanging loosely by his side. To avoid catching the horse's side while feeling for the irons, the rider's feet should be placed in them by the trainer. Thereafter before mounting the leathers should be twisted to let the irons hang at right angles to the horse's side.

Dismounting

Feeling his rider dismount for the first time can be a frightening experience for the young horse. The sudden alteration of weight may alarm him. The impression that he has of this final part of the lesson will be uppermost in his mind when he returns to the stable, so it is important to avoid a drama. Once the halt and standstill are established, the rider should gently ease his feet out of the irons, so that they do not bang the horse's sides. He should take the reins in the left hand, hold the neck strap and lean slowly forward. Then he should quietly swing his right leg over the horse's back and slide down in a steady continuous movement, rather than jump off suddenly with a thud. The horse must not think that a sudden movement by the rider means – no rider!

Once the rider's right leg is over the horse's back, he must continue to dismount, even if the horse makes a sudden movement. Any attempt to cling on or to climb back will frighten the horse more. At this point it is better to ignore the horse's tension than to prolong it. If dismounting is carried out as described, and if an issue is not made of it, the horse will soon learn to stand in a relaxed way.

The period during which the young horse is backed is not only physically but also mentally tiring for him. Two work sessions per day, possibly of twenty minutes each, are of greater benefit than one longer session, for during the break the horse goes back to the secure surroundings of his stable and thinks about his lesson. If it has been well planned and executed there should be no need for him to worry.

8

Riding Away

The young horse will now have reached the stage when he will accept the rider on his back. He will stand or walk calmly forward, carrying his rider, while being led and controlled by his trainer. He will be learning to balance his rider's weight as well as his own.

Soon a few strides of trot will be introduced, at first on a straight line with the rider sitting softly in balance, without tension. The horse should be given time to rebalance and settle down in walk before being asked to trot again. In the early days after backing, he will not normally be asked to carry the rider for more than ten to fifteen minutes twice a day. As his balance improves and his muscles develop, work periods may be extended perhaps to half an hour.

Teaching the horse the aids
At this point, the horse is controlled by the voice and the movements of his trainer, on the ground. Now he must learn

to accept control from the rider on his back. This is achieved by introducing the rider's aids (signals) in conjunction with those of the trainer.

At first the horse may not understand that the leg aid means 'go forward', but if, at the same moment, the trainer says 'Walk on' and walks forward, the horse will associate the commands and will gradually learn to move forward from the rider's leg. If the horse jumps forward suddenly, the rider must, if necessary, use the neck strap rather than restore his balance by pulling on the reins.

The rider should use an allowing, following hand, and should guide the horse in the required direction with an 'open rein' (Fig. 21). His rein aids should also be introduced by using them with the trainer's appropriate voice aid and movement. The horse should accept the feel of the reins, as he will have been lunged with side reins earlier in his training. The rider

Fig. 21 Using an 'open rein'.

will soon use his own voice to reassure the horse and to confirm leg and rein aids when necessary. He should use the same words and intonation as the trainer. Gradually he will begin to control the horse. How long this takes to achieve will depend on how well the horse responds and on the skill and experience of the rider.

Working towards independence from the trainer

As the rider's influence increases, the trainer will take a more passive role. He may gradually move away from the horse, gently letting out the lunge line, and taking almost a lungeing position, so that the horse learns to walk out on his own. The horse can then proceed to walking several yards away from the trainer, turning wide corners while the trainer stands still. Soon the rider will be able to halt, walk and trot the horse without help from the trainer.

Once the horse and rider are confidently performing easy turns, large circles and transitions in walk and trot – away from the trainer, but still on the lunge line – the cavesson and lunge line may be removed. The trainer's presence will continue to provide a reassuring influence.

Work in the schooling area

Over a period of days or even weeks, work should continue in the schooling area until the horse fully understands and responds to the aids. Care must be taken not to overtax either his body or his mind. The rider should therefore ride him on a long rein, encouraging him to go forward in a relaxed, free and supple way. He must be allowed to find his own balance. Aids should be deliberate, clear and definite.

In these early days, the horse will not be able to work as a mature horse might, using precise movements and small circles. Instead, he must learn to work forward and straight. Transitions may take several strides; smoothness is more important than accuracy.

Turns and circles must be wide and large so that he can be asked to move with a slight but uniform bend through his body. He should be encouraged to develop his balance while moving in a free and rhythmical way. The rider must bear in mind his horse's lack of strength and co-ordination.

Be aware of how the horse's mind is working. Like a child, he will experiment to see what is acceptable and what is not. The rider must provide tactful but firm answers. *The horse must not be allowed to get the upper hand.* Work should be hard enough to warrant concentration, but not hard enough to cause frustration. The rider should keep the horse 'thinking forward'.

Remember to change direction occasionally, and when working in rising trot, change the diagonal appropriately, so that the horse's muscles develop in an even way.

Once the rider is confident that he can control the horse in walk and trot, he should try a few strides of canter. The horse will already have cantered without the rider on the lunge (see page 71). His first canter strides with a rider will be easier if they are carried out on a straight line. Remember that most horses will not be able to canter a 20-metre circle for some time. They will lose their balance if their work is made too difficult too soon. This will cause loss of confidence and will spoil the freedom of the strides.

When the horse is reasonably obedient, schooling can be carried out in a variety of areas, such as the corner of a flat field or any safe, suitable place where the going is sound and not heavy. This will help to extend his experience.

The result of the work, at this stage, should be an obedient, confident, happy horse who complies with his rider's wishes and is able to walk, trot and canter in a calm unhurried way on either rein in a large schooling area, using long, straight lines, wide easy turns and very large circles.

Riding away from the schooling area

On the first few occasions when you venture outside the schooling area, choose familiar places – perhaps the stable or farmyard, or the back drive with the gate at the end closed. Ride up and down or round about, making many transitions and asking the horse to stand still at times. Without his trainer leading him, many everyday sights and smells may seem suddenly frightening to the youngster. His first instinct will be to turn and run. Try to avoid this by reassuring him with your voice, and *allowing him time to look* while preventing him from turning, so that he can face and accept the problem. With his rider giving him confidence and encouragement he should then walk on past. Reward him briefly for moving forward, and make as little as possible of the incident.

While riding out on your youngster, it is sensible to wear a brightly coloured bib with 'CAUTION: YOUNG HORSE' on it.

A sensible companion

Another rider with a quiet, reliable horse will be a reassuring influence and will be especially useful when you are ready to go further afield, during early days on the road, and in the future at horse shows and out cub-hunting. It is best to use a horse which the youngster knows well: perhaps a former field companion, or a horse which has previously shared the schooling area. On some days the young horse should work on his own, on others the older horse's presence can be used for reassurance and to teach the young one how to behave in company. There is a danger that the young horse might become too dependent on his 'nanny' and unwilling to go forward alone. Therefore, once the two horses are settled working side by side, the older horse might drop back slightly and allow the young horse to lead for a while, or perhaps stand still while the young horse is ridden back and forth past him. The type of day, the environment, and how the young horse feels, will determine how much progress you can ask for and how much independence you can expect.

Fig. 22 Fluent and careful over a single pole.

Undulating ground

Once the horse is carrying you in a reasonably balanced way on flat ground, he can be ridden up and down slopes and on different types of going. This will help to develop his balance further and teach him to be sure-footed.

Varying the work

While out hacking, the horse will meet a variety of new experiences. He should be expected to look at, and then move forward over, small logs and ditches which he meets while out on exercise.

Work will continue in the schooling area, and the horse will be learning to walk and trot over a single pole on the ground (Fig. 22), and then over more poles at the correct distance apart for the length of his trotting stride (see page 93). Lungeing will be continued as a useful alternative, especially to settle the horse before riding him after a rest day.

Traffic will first be met at home in the safety of a controlled situation.

9

Teaching the Horse to Jump

The horse should be taught to jump as part of his general education. He will be a better ride if he learns from the early stages to look where he is going, and to negotiate small obstacles which are in his path. First, he will learn to walk over a pole on the ground in a calm and careful way, while he is being led. Later, he will be expected to negotiate poles and small logs while being ridden. Before he learns to jump smoothly, he will probably leave the ground in a rather unco-ordinated way. At this time it is vital for the rider not to add to his problems by further unbalancing him or catching him in the mouth. Therefore, early lessons in jumping are best taught on the lunge without a rider.

Lungeing over fences

Use a flat, enclosed area where the going is true and not heavy. Before the horse is lunged over fences, he must be obedient on the lunge and you must be proficient enough to control him on circles and straight lines while lungeing. You must be able to move the position of the horse's circle in a tactful way without upsetting the rhythm of his trot. The correct position of the lunger is the key to controlling the horse. You must be agile enough to retain your position so that the horse is always in front of you, controlled between your whip (leg) and lunge line (hand). The horse must not be allowed to think that he can refuse or run out. You must be able to settle him in a balanced active trot from which to approach the fence and continue the exercise.

Place a pole on the ground, at right-angles to a substantial wall or fence, with a pair of small stands positioned ready to make a jump. Take a second pole and use it as a wing, from the top of the inside stand to the ground. This will also act as a 'runner' for the lunge line (Figs. 23a and 24).

Use the normal lungeing equipment, but do not use side reins for jumping.

It is helpful to have an assistant who can move the poles and build the jump.

Begin lungeing as usual, working the horse on both reins at walk and trot. Then lead him over the pole at the walk. Allow him to look and walk on calmly between the stands and over the pole without hurrying. When he is managing this without any fuss, lunge him at the trot, taking position A, shown in Figure 25, with the horse circling round you. Then move gradually to position B with the horse moving on to its circle and then, through position C, on to position and circle D. From there you will be able to move to position E, while the horse, during one circuit, moves on to the track, which will necessitate him trotting over the pole. You must be confident that you can do this in a way that leaves the horse in no doubt

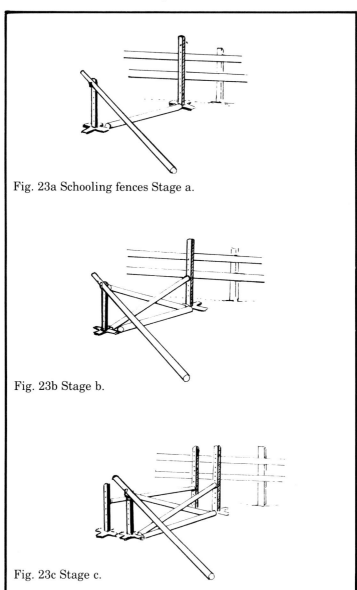

Fig. 23a Schooling fences Stage a.

Fig. 23b Stage b.

Fig. 23c Stage c.

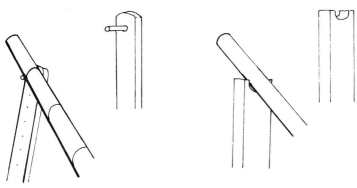

Fig. 24 Two ways to build a 'Runner'.

as to whether he is expected to circle on the near side of the wing or to go on over the pole.

While he is trotting over the pole, you should be calmly but quickly maintaining your position from E to F, moving parallel with him, so that he is able to move freely forward in a

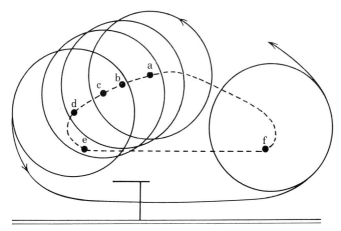

Fig. 25 The tracks to be followed when jumping a horse on the lunge.

straight line before gradually turning on to a circle. While he is on the straight line, there should be some slack in the lunge line. He should remain settled while you return to position A.

Once you have the horse trotting calmly over the pole, you can build a small jump of cross-poles behind it (Fig. 23b). Proceed, as before, from position A through positions B, C and D to position E. The approach should always be made in trot, and since the horse might land in canter, you will need to move quickly to follow him, and settle him in the trot, moving gently back to position A before repeating the exercise.

Some horses find jumping easy from the beginning, others will need time and practice to jump confidently (Fig. 26).

Fig. 26 Jumping on the lunge.

Remember the following:
☐ Use your voice not only to control the horse, but to reassure him and to praise him when he has negotiated the obstacle, however awkwardly he does this in the initial stages.
☐ Work on both reins.
☐ Do not continue jumping for too long.
☐ Use your discretion to end the lesson at a sensible moment when the horse has produced a good jump which was comfort-

able for him. This may be achieved quite quickly after one or two jumps, or it may take a few more. Patient repetition will improve some horses: but settle for a modest improvement rather than continuing until the horse tires and his work deteriorates.

During later lessons, the jump may be made into a small spread fence (Fig. 23c) which can then be enlarged slightly in height and width, although it is better to increase its spread rather than its height.

Your aim should always be to promote calm, purposeful work, increasing the horse's confidence by revising and building on each lesson, and reverting to previous ones to make corrections if things go wrong.

Riding the horse over poles on the ground (Fig. 27)
Trotting over poles on the ground is a most useful exercise. It should be introduced as part of his ridden work while the horse is at the stage when he is learning to jump on the lunge. He should be ridden on a long rein with a following hand.

The horse should be familiar with being ridden over single poles placed at random on the ground, at walk and rising trot. Once an active rhythmical trot has been established, he should be ridden over two poles on the ground, with approximately 9ft (2.7m) between them. Then a third should be added in the centre, making approximately 4ft 6ins (1.35m) between each pole. When he is trotting over these calmly and confidently, and when you have made any adjustments to the distances, a fourth can be added at a similar distance.

The poles will:
☐ Improve the quality of the trot.
☐ Encourage him to stretch and round his back as he looks down to see and avoid them by stepping over them.
☐ Regulate the length and rhythm of his stride, which will improve his balance.
☐ Improve his co-ordination.

Fig. 27 Carrying his rider calmly over a series of poles.

☐ Help in the correct development of the muscles of the shoulders and hindquarters due to increased activity.

If the exercise is performed correctly, the horse will be encouraged to use joints and muscles to an increased extent and it will then become very hard work. Care must be taken not to overtax the horse and so do more harm than good.

94

The principles of jumping

Before riding the young horse over fences, you must be confident that you will not interfere with him while he jumps. Any alterations or adjustments to the pace must be made early in the approach, after which the rider's purpose is to maintain an unhurried, confident progress towards, over, and away from the fence, encouraging the horse to jump in a natural, relaxed and calm way. You must be proficient enough to stay in balance so that you do not interfere with his efforts to use his head, neck and body. The rider who loses his balance may accidently punish the horse for jumping by burdening the horse's loins or by catching him in the mouth. Even the most experienced rider will use a neck strap as a safeguard at this stage.

The horse should be encouraged to jump as efficiently as he can, using minimum effort for maximum achievement. To analyse how this is done, the jump is normally divided into five phases:

(a) The approach.
(b) The take-off.
(c) The period of suspension.
(d) The landing.
(e) The get-away (or recovery).

Fig. 28a The phases of the jump – Approach.

During the approach the horse lowers his head and stretches his neck. This enables him to balance himself and prepare to make his jump.

95

Fig. 28b Take-off.

As he takes off he shortens his neck slightly, raises his head, and lifts his forehand off the ground. He then brings his hocks under him, and, as his hind feet touch the ground, he stretches his head and neck, and uses the power of his hindquarters to spring forward and upward.

Fig. 28c Period of suspension.

During the period of suspension the head and neck are stretched forwards and downwards to their fullest extent, enabling the front legs to be tucked up. The hind legs, having left the ground, follow the parabola of the body.

Fig. 28d Landing.

As the horse lands his head comes up and his neck shortens. His forelegs touch down one after the other, followed by the hind legs.

Fig. 28e Get-away (or recovery).

During the get-away (or recovery) the horse rebalances and re-establishes the trot or canter.

All horses, and especially young ones, should enjoy jumping. The rider must not spoil this enjoyment.

Riding over fences

When the horse has learned to jump smoothly on the lunge and to trot calmly over four or five poles on the ground while carrying his rider, he can be ridden over a small jump from the trot. Use the same single obstacle which he has been jumping on the lunge (Figure 23b). At first it should be small, just high enough to necessitate jumping it rather than trotting over it. This will be the horse's first attempt to balance the weight of his rider in addition to his own, while he jumps. It is therefore most important for the rider to sit quietly and in balance. Most horses need time and practice before they will leave the ground confidently while carrying the extra weight of the rider (Fig. 29).

If the horse shows signs of hurrying or of losing balance in the approach, circle away, re-establish the trot, and then try again. A rushed approach is a sign of tension, not enthusiasm. It may be necessary to return to the 'trotting poles'. Foundations laid now will influence the horse's attitude to

Fig. 29 His first jump with a rider – leaving the ground in an unco-ordinated way.

jumping for the future. Be patient, and give him time to learn to jump confidently.

Being a normal part of every horse's basic education, jumping should be integrated into the work programme on several occasions each week.

Over a period of months, as the horse's balance improves and his muscles develop, his jumping should become smooth, deliberate and competent.

When the horse has developed a balanced canter on the flat, you can allow him to canter the last one or two strides before the fence. If this excites him, go back to trot, establish calmness in trot and canter on the flat, and try again. Progress towards the complete approach in canter will depend on each individual.

The horse should have plenty of practice over fences of not more than about 2ft 9ins (0.8m) high and wide. In the first year, the fences should remain at about these sizes. If the horse is over-faced, he will soon learn to refuse. Instead of increasing the size, introduce variety: banks; little walls; coloured poles; wet, dry and blind ditches; doubles; trebles;

Fig. 30 Becoming more competent – compare this with Fig. 29, opposite.

fences up and down hills; and drops. Include as many spread fences – tree trunks, parallel poles and ditches – as uprights. Schooling fences should look substantial. The horse should not find out that it is easier to knock them down than to adjust his stride when meeting a fence 'wrong'. Small tree trunks which cannot roll are ideal at this stage (Fig. 30).

Sensible progress will result in a trusting, confident horse who will jump any fence at which he is presented, intelligently and happily. Once this has been achieved, he will be ready to compete in small (minimus) cross-country and show-jumping competitions. He will have learned the mechanics of jumping and should continue to improve as he matures and his all-round training progresses.

10

Widening the Horse's Experience

Your aim so far will have been to produce a four-year-old who is unblemished in mind and body. The backing and riding away will have been completed, but the horse is still in his formative years and will be quick to react to the way he is handled. The manner in which he is ridden and schooled will determine his progress towards becoming a balanced, forward-going ride.

Circles and other movements must be performed in both directions. The horse must learn to be equally comfortable with his rider sitting on either diagonal in rising trot. He must be helped to develop his muscles equally on both sides so that he is able to perform easily in either direction. He must learn to balance himself during transitions so that they become smooth and are performed without resistance. His jumping should become more competent with practice and as his balance improves.

Obedience should now be established in a variety of different circumstances.

In the stable

From the early stages the horse should be taught respect for and obedience to his trainer. Good manners must be insisted upon, both in and out of the stable. Remember that manners, good and bad, are catching. If yours are uncouth and impatient your horse's will be the same. For example, when first trimming or clipping, a firm but patient approach is required with plenty of time available.

When pulling the mane and tail, take out only a few hairs at a time until the horse accepts what you are doing. To avoid soreness, pull the mane and tail gradually, achieving the required length or shape over a period of time. Preferably, work for short periods just after his exercise, as he should then be relaxed and his pores will be open. While being careful not to cause unnecessary discomfort, be firm and insist that the horse stands still.

Before clipping a young horse it is important for him to stand in a relaxed manner while the clipping machine is operating. At first, run it outside his stable, moving nearer as he becomes used to the noise. The amount of time needed before he is relaxed while the clippers are running near to his body will depend on his character and training. A low trace-clip, omitting the head and neck, would be a sensible introduction. An efficient machine and sharp blades are essential. If you take care to prevent a nick, discomfort from hot blades, or blades which pull the hair, the young horse will soon accept clipping in the same way as he does grooming. (See the Pony Club *Manual of Horsemanship* for advice on clipping.)

On the road

In many areas, riding on the road is hazardous, and it is very difficult to educate a horse amid fast traffic and inconsiderate drivers. If possible, he should spend some time turned out in a safely fenced field next to a busy road. This will accustom him to the sight and sound of heavy traffic; he will have seen local traffic throughout his education. If your immediate roads are too busy it may be necessary to box him to quiet country lanes for a while.

When he is first ridden on the road, an experienced companion should accompany him, to provide a reassuring influence. The older horse should be ridden on the outside and slightly ahead of him. As the novice becomes more confident, he will be able to draw alongside the other horse, and, at times be slightly ahead.

Most horses are quite sensible in traffic unless they have been frightened. Noisy vehicles, air brakes, or spray on rainy days can cause a shock which has a lasting effect. Try to introduce these from a distance and then gradually from closer proximity. Over a period of time, the horse should become confident while being ridden nearer to traffic, and as long as his temperament allows, he should become steady on the road either alone or ahead of other horses.

Travelling in a horsebox or trailer

A young horse who has been taken out a few times with his dam while he was a foal will have an advantage over the horse who has never left home. However, travelling seldom presents a problem providing that certain precautions are taken on the first few occasions when the horse is asked to load, travel and unload. Travelling is fully covered in the Pony Club *Manual of Horsemanship*. With the young horse, the following additional points must be taken into account:

☐ Large horses generally travel better in horseboxes than in trailers. Horseboxes are more roomy and inviting for loading,

103

although some have very steep ramps, which must be made more accessible by dropping them on to raised ground. A large step at the top of a ramp may also cause a problem. Ramps without gates should not be used.

☐ Allow much more time than you think is necessary.

☐ The first time, load directly from the stable if this is possible. Alternatively choose a quiet place which has natural boundaries.

☐ Prepare the box in advance. Have any necessary aids, such as a lungeing line, ready.

☐ It is a help to use another horse who will load well, to give a lead into the box, and to act as a travelling companion.

☐ For better control, use a lungeing cavesson. Do not travel a young horse with a saddle on.

Treat the whole exercise in a calm, relaxed manner, as your attitude will influence the horse.

The first introductory lesson should conclude after the horse has settled in the box. Give him a small feed before unloading him. Repeat this lesson for several days at a time.

The next stage is to take the horse on a short, easy journey.

Particular care must be taken when driving a box, and even more so with a trailer, which has a whiplash effect. Braking must be gentle; corners must be taken steadily. Always remember that your horse is a movable cargo and can be thrown off balance.

The motion experienced inside the horsebox or trailer is very different from that in the driver's seat. It is worth trying it yourself in an empty vehicle to gauge the effect.

A horse which has had difficulty staying on his feet will arrive in a state of nervous panic and may never travel well again. If the first few journeys are pleasant, the horse will soon accept travelling as a normal part of life.

When you arrive at your destination, give him time to look about before unloading.

Calm confidence on your part and a sensible amount of time allowed at every stage – loading, driving, settling down – will pay dividends.

Out and about

Once the young horse has been ridden away and is settled in his behaviour, the next step is to take him to his first outing.

If he has been shown occasionally as a youngster, he should be accustomed to the sights and sounds of a competition environment. Yet however well you know a young horse, you can never be certain as to exactly how he will react. It is most important to prepare him so that he can enjoy his first 'party'. This will give both him and his rider confidence. Set-backs at this stage may have lasting results.

A small event where there will be plenty of space, and an unhurried atmosphere is ideal: a Pony Club rally, a small show, or a hunter trial not too far away from home would probably be the most suitable. He should attend, but not compete at, these early outings. Early mornings out cub-hunting accompanied by a well-mannered horse can be very beneficial; they can offer long, quiet exercise with the time and space to learn about new sights and sounds. Several mornings may be needed for a young horse to become used to the excitement and to learn patience on such occasions.

Make sure that the horse is well worked for several days before his outing. It would be unwise to take him after a day off, when he may be fresh and full of himself. Some horses may benefit from being worked on the same morning before they leave home. If the event is within hacking distance it may be advisable to ride there, as this will help to settle the horse.

Travelling with an older horse who is competing is one way of getting the young horse out and about, but standing for a long time in the horsebox can upset some animals. The young horse should not be allowed to make a nuisance of himself by stamping or scraping on the floor of the vehicle. The more time spent outside the better – perhaps hand-grazing him or leading him around for part of the day.

105

All of these early outings are important training sessions. The aim is to acquaint the young horse with the outside world, so that he will accept it without becoming worried or excited, while remaining obedient.

Do not expect, or try to do, anything with your young horse that you have not already achieved at home.

To this stage his education will have been strenuous, both mentally and physically. Once he is established and correct in his way of going, at home and in company, he will benefit from a rest. Allow a four- to six-week break, during which the horse will have time to absorb what he has learned, and should then return to work refreshed.

His temperament, attitude and physical strength, and the experience of his rider will determine his progress towards whatever objective has been chosen for him in the future.

The joy of riding a well-trained horse, who is able to use his natural ability to its best advantage, will make all your time and effort worthwhile.

Index

A

Afterbirth *see* Placenta
Aids 79, 81-83
   see also Commands, Voice
Areas
   for backing 74
   for foaling 18
   for introducing new equipment 47
   for loading 104
   for lungeing 62-63
   for lungeing over fences 89
   for mares and foals 13-14
   for riding away 85, 87
   for schooling 84
Assistants 35, 37, 39-40, 47-48,
   68-70, 75-76, 89

B

Backing 72-80
   area for 74
   equipment for 73
   preliminaries to 74-78
   time required for 72
Balance 12, 59, 81, 84, 89, 93, 95,
   99, 102
Behaviour, equine 9-10
Bits 45, 53-54, 64, 66
Boots 46, 50, 53, 59, 68, 73
Bran mash 18, 23-24
Breast girth 47-49, 54, 57, 68
Breast-plate 57, 68, 73
Breeding 13-24
   facilities required 13
   foaling 18-24
   mare for 14-15
   sending mare to stud 15-17
   signs of pregnancy 17-18

stallion 13, 15
Bridles 53-55, 71, 73

C

Canter 71, 84, 99
Carbohydrates 28
Castrating (gelding) 42, 46
Cavesson (lungeing) 45, 56-57, 68,
   73, 104
Circles 59, 66, 71, 83-84, 89, 101
Cleansing 22
Clipping and trimming 102
Clothing (human) 44, 59
Colostrum 23
Colts 44, 46
Commands 33, 37, 39, 44-45, 61,
   64, 68, 70, 79
   see also Aids, Voice
Companion 10, 41-42, 85, 103-104
Concentrated feeds 26-28
Contact 45, 57, 59, 69
   see also Rein aids
Crupper 57

D

Diagonals 84, 101
Dismounting 80

E

Education
   of foals 32-40
   of yearlings 44-45
   of two-year-olds 46-47
   of three-year-olds 52-53
Elements *see* Minerals
Equipment
   check list for foaling 23-24

for backing 73
for lungeing 55-59
introducing new 46

F
Facilities *see* Areas
Farrier 39, 43
  see also Feet
Feeding 25-31
  essential nutrients 28-31
  principles of 27-28
Feet 45
  see also Farrier
Fences *see* Jumping
Fencing 14, 37
Fields 14, 17, 37, 39, 41, 62, 74
  see also Grazing
Fillies 46
Foaling 13-14, 18-24
Foals 14, 22-26, 32-42
  breeding 14, 22-24
  education of 32-40
  handling of 33-42
  new born 22-24
  physiology 25-26
  psychology 33
  weaning 41
  veterinary attention 42
Foal slips 35-36, 38
Four-year-old 101

G
Gelding (castrating) 42, 46
Gestation period 16
Grazing 13, 26
  see also Fields
Ground poles *see* Poles, ground

H
Hacking 87, 105
Halting 39, 45, 64, 67-68, 70, 80-81
  see also Standing still
Hay 26, 28
Headcollar 16, 45, 53
  see also Foal slip

Horsebox 103-105
Hunting 10, 85, 105

I
Immunisation 16, 23, 42
Influenza *see* Immunisation
Instinct 11

J
Jumping 88-100, 102
  on the lunge 89-93
  phases of the jump 95-97
  poles (ground) 53, 87, 93-94
  preliminaries to 53, 87
  principles of 95-97
  riding over fences 98-100
  schooling fences 88-93, 99-100

L
Lactation *see* Milk
Laminitis 29
Leading in hand
  before lungeing 58-69
  foals 33, 36-38
  yearlings 44-45
  two-year-olds 46
Loading *see* Travelling
Loosebox 14, 74
Lungeing 55-72, 74-75, 78, 87,
  89-93
  aims 59
  control 61
  equipment for 55-59
  leading before 68-69
  method when 64
  over jumps 89-93
  purposes of 55
  teaching a horse 67-71
  two-year-olds 50
  three-year-olds 54
Lunge line 45, 57, 73
  holding the 63-64
Lunger 59-71
  clothing for 59
  position of 62-63

M

Mane 44
  pulling 102
Manners 9, 11, 34, 39, 45, 52, 102
Mare, brood *see* Breeding
Meconium 23
Memory 10
Milk 23, 26, 29
Minerals 29-30
Mouth 9, 52, 53
Muzzle 9, 11
  see also Nose

N

'Nanny' horse *see* Companion
National Foaling Bank 24
Neck strap 73, 78, 80, 82, 95
Nose 45, 70
  see also Muzzle
Nutrients 28

O

Outline 60-61, 71

P

Peristalsis 27
Physiology
  of foals 25-26
  of yearlings 44
  of two-year-olds 45
  of three-year-olds 50-51
Placenta 22-24
Ponies (small) 9, 13, 17-18, 28, 29
Poles 89-91
  ground 53, 87, 93-94
Pregnancy *see* Breeding
Proteins 28-29
Psychology 8-10
  of foals 33
  of yearlings 44
  of two-year-olds 46
  of three-year-olds 52
Pulling, mane and tail 102

R

Rein 55, 80, 82
  'open' 82-83

side 57-60, 64, 66-67, 71
  see also Lunge line
Rein aids 82-83
  see also Contact
Riding away 81-87
  companion for 85
  in the schooling area 83-84
  out of the schooling area 83-87
  teaching of the aids 82-83
Road, on the *see* Traffic
Rollers 47-50, 54, 57, 68
Roughage 27-28
Rugs 46-50

S

Saddles 48, 53-54, 57, 71, 73, 76, 78-79
Salt lick 26, 29
Schooling 83-87, 101
Scouring (foal) 23
Season, mare in 16-17, 23
Side reins 57-59, 64, 66
Stable *see* Loosebox
Stable rubber 36-38
Stallion *see* Breeding
Standing still 10-11, 39, 80, 85
  see also Halting
Stirrups 58, 75, 78-79
Stud *see* Breeding
Swab tests 15-16

T

Tail 44, 67, 79
  pulling 102
Teeth 52-53
Temperament 14-15, 78, 103, 106
Tetanus *see* Immunisation
Three-year-olds 50-54, 73
  education of 52-53
  introducing new equipment 53-54
  physiology 50-52
  psychology 52
Traffic 40, 53, 87, 103
Trailer 103-105
Trainer, characteristics of 7-8

Transitions 64, 83, 85, 102
Travelling 40-41, 103-105
Trot 39, 64, 67, 70-71, 81, 84, 89,
  93, 98, 101
Trotting poles *see* Poles, ground
'Turning in', on lunge 62, 66
Turning out, mare and foal 37-39
Two-year-olds 45-50
  education of 52-53
  introducing new equipment 46-50
  physiology 44
  psychology 44
Tying up
  foals 39-40
  yearlings 45
  three-year-olds 52

U
Umbilical cord 22, 24

V
Venereal diseases 16

Veterinary attention 39, 42
Vices, stable 10
Vitamins 30-31
Voice 23, 32, 48, 61, 64, 66, 68,
  70, 75, 78, 81
  see also Aids, Commands

W
Walk 38-39, 67, 70, 81-82, 89
Water 8, 14, 23, 26-27
Weaning 27, 41-42
Whip 44, 68
  lungeing 57, 61, 63-69, 89
Wild horses 8
Worming 16, 24, 42-43

Y
Yearlings 41, 43-45
  education 44-45
  physiology 44
  psychology 44